ABCs for
Dementia
Caregivers

ABCs for Dementia Caregivers

A HANDBOOK FOR CAREGIVERS

PATRICE GAPEN AND MICHAEL HAND

Archway Publishing books may be ordered through booksellers or by contacting:

Archway Publishing
1663 Liberty Drive
Bloomington, IN 47403
www.archwaypublishing.com
844-669-3957

ISBN: 978-1-6657-3599-5 (sc)
ISBN: 978-1-6657-3598-8 (hc)
ISBN: 978-1-6657-3600-8 (e)

Library of Congress Control Number: 2022923877

Print information available on the last page.

Archway Publishing rev. date: 04/26/2023

We dedicate this work to our beloved spouses, Frank and Terry, who taught us what it means to love unconditionally.

We also dedicate this text to the unsung heroes of dementia, the families of those afflicted with this terrible disease.

CONTENTS

AUTHORS' NOTE

We wish we could have reached you sooner. If you are reading this, you may already be in crisis. You are carrying a burden no one else understands down a path that seemingly leads nowhere. All the while you are doing this, the person you are helping is getting in the way, asking the same questions over and over, and generally making your life miserable.

We have been there. We understand. We know there is nothing we can do across the miles or across the years to reduce your burden. However, we can offer some practical bits of advice.

One of the biggest issues we learned during our journey is that denial is real. We both denied our spouses' conditions for entirely too long before we began to take many of the steps in this book. Did we do everything right? Absolutely not! Would we do things differently again? Absolutely! Would we want to do it again? If you have to ask that, you have not lived with a person who has dementia or another other debilitating disease.

We should have been quicker to acknowledge the little signs. Some of the things we noticed but did not acknowledge were the lack of attention to their appearance, that ever so slight loss of concentration, and the small messes in the bedroom, bathroom, or kitchen. Each of our reactions was generally, "That is not like them," ignoring the incident and moving on.

We wish we had done more sooner. But like you may have done, we ignored, we denied, we delayed. We thought our loved ones were just going through a rough patch. What we missed was that the rough patch was the start of a long, slow, shared process that would ultimately result in the passing of our loved ones.

We thought this kind of thing happened to other people, not to us. Welcome to the club no one wants to join. We are sorry that you have joined our club. At times you will wonder if you can make it. We know you can as we, too, have endured.

GRAMMATICAL NOTE

The use of male or female pronouns is not intended to be discriminatory. They are used to improve the flow of the text. Except for personal stories, "they" or "them" refers to the person with dementia, while "he," "him," "man," "she," "her," or "woman" refers to the caregiver or a member of the caregiving team. The pronoun "you" can refer to the reader or any member of the family or caregiving team.

INTRODUCTION

This is a book for the one who is not yet left behind. You may be the one no one notices because your husband/wife/partner/parent/other significant person is still alive. Taking care of your beloved takes all your time and energy. Yet, you are not single; you are not free to socialize or travel. You are not divorced and free of the financial burdens of doctor's fees, costs for modifications to the house or of the time commitments to care for them. Their care is your responsibility.

But your relationship with them has changed. If they were your spouse, you are not really married any longer. There are no Christmas parties you can both attend, no more traveling, no ability to dance and enjoy the band at the club, no companionship, no help with decisions, no one to talk to at night. Intimacy is gone.

If the afflicted is your parent, your roles have reversed. You must now look out for them. Rather than have them look out for you, drive you to functions or to doctor's appointments, these duties become your responsibility. You are still their child, and they still think of you as an underling. However, now you must make difficult decisions for them. These can be decisions about trying a new medication, modifying their house, or selling their car. And you must ultimately consider your parents' demise.

There is no wish to devalue the loss of a significant other. The twenty-first century has brought many advances in medical technology. Many diseases from years past that were inoperable or untreatable are now cured, treated, or managed. Lifetimes have been extended ten, twenty, or thirty years. Within the span of a generation, the death of someone who was close to us was the biggest loss one could experience. Today, the greatest loss may be when the people closest to us do not die but linger.

This is not a how-to manual. Neither is it a medical reference book nor a book of legal advice. However, the stories and suggestions should help the patient and the caregiver. These are what the authors found worked for them. For the same reasons every person and every relationship is different, everyone experiencing these situations has different things to deal with. To that end, you will not find long passages of philosophy with beautifully polished sentences. This is a much more practical book with short paragraphs, concise chapters, and we hope useful suggestions for events you may encounter. This is because both authors know that there is no single solution for every situation.

Take the few minutes you have for yourself, scan the "Contents," and know that you are not the only one dealing with these situations.

If there is one takeaway from this book it is this:

"As long as you take care of them with a caring soul
and love in your heart, you are doing the right thing."

Take what helps from our book and find your own solutions for the rest of your situation. We wish you all the best.

CHAPTER 1

The Adult You Fell in Love With

We didn't realize back then that we got such a gem for a spouse. And who knew back when we said, "I do," that our spouses could make our life turn from black and white to technicolor?

That special person who lights up your life.

Those feelings were all the love and affection we could ever want or need. We had the confidence that whatever life threw at us, we were a team, and together could handle anything. With our spouse at our side, as a couple we were more than we ever were alone. We doubled or tripled our confidence and abilities! We knew that this person made us better than we ever were or would be without them.

And then it happened. With the diagnosis of dementia, everything came crashing down. For some, it crashes like a bunker-buster bomb. For others, recognition comes slower. Like a glacier, a few small pieces melting over time, running slowly down the slope, it is virtually imperceptible until something happens, something that changes everything.

Alan was in denial about Abby's dementia until she called the police to report that he was having an affair and strangers were in the house.

Abby was raised in a military family, widely traveled, multilingual. More than that, she was a hostess extraordinaire who made everyone laugh with wonderful, quick-witted jokes while serving four-course dinners. She worked all her life as a teacher with a master's degree. But more than that, she was Alan's loving wife for the thirty-nine years she was his soul mate. Alan did not notice her slow decline. When Alan did notice, he wrote it off to fatigue or advancing age. It wasn't until the car accident that Alan started to wonder.

Bob told his new wife that his foot wasn't working. He was attempting to climb the stairs in their multilevel home to join her for dinner, but he recognized he couldn't make it up to the dining room.

Bob was a "man's man." According to one of his friends, Bob had done everything in the world … twice. Growing up poor in the Midwest, he showed mechanical aptitude at a young age. This, combined with his gregarious personality, led him to drag racing on highways at night, usually bringing home a pocketful of cash. When his country called him, he gladly stepped forward. His public service record was amazing. He spent thirty-one years serving his country on six continents and forty-three countries. This included service in Vietnam. His claim to fame there was that he spent two years flying combat missions and came home without a scratch. He did this while raising a son and a daughter alongside his wife.

After his service in the military, he and his wife built a successful retail business that they maintained until she died of cancer. Taking care of his wife until her death at home left him with great grief and loss. He tried to move on, but the grief wouldn't leave. He moved out of state and remarried. A few years later, he was diagnosed with dementia. His new wife was handed an abundance of medical issues, financial questions, two stepchildren, and a flood of problems and a medical history that she had never known.

Carl was a typical spouse. He loved his wife, Cathy, and they built a wonderful life and family together.

Cathy was a lovely, energetic, sweet person. She met Carl at the local church right after high school. She laughed easily and was quick with comebacks. When they were first married, Carl loved her even more when she brought her homegrown flowers for his mother. She got a job at the local grocery store and started stocking shelves. After they got married, Cathy was promoted to cashier. Cashier was the "cherry" job with easier work and more money. The extra money came in handy when she got pregnant. After the baby came, she went back to work part time while grandma watched the baby. Carl was in seventh heaven; everything was picture perfect. When baby number two came along, he thought he couldn't be happier. Cathy quit work at the grocery store to take care of the children. She became the perfect housekeeper, cook, and room mother.

Cathy is a typical example of early-onset dementia. Ten years later, Carl was faced with this situation.

Cathy started dinner and then decided to go out and weed the flower bed. After all, it was a beautiful, lovely day with just the perfect weather. But later, Carl got a call from the kids. Cathy hadn't picked them up from soccer practice. Carl had to leave work early, with a caustic comment from the boss. The coaches were grouchy when he got to the practice field. Waiting for Carl had made them late for their dinners. The kids were hungry, crabby, and angry about having to wait around so long. When Carl got home, the house was filled with smoke, and the alarms were screaming. Scared, the kids joined in the screaming. They knew smoke wasn't normal, and they couldn't find their mom. They were terrified that something had happened to her. Cathy heard the commotion and came running to find out what was going on. Cathy got the kids settled while Carl took the smoking dinner outside and hosed it down. That night, Carl tried to talk to Cathy about what happened. Cathy's frustration and guilt over what happened turned ugly. Rather than admit to Carl that she didn't remember starting dinner, Cathy became belligerent. She started to list all of Carl's flaws, beginning with something that happened when they were dating, mistakes he made when they were first married, and how his job had moved them away from her parents! When Carl kept trying to figure out what had happened with the burning dinner, Cathy got nastier, saying, "Well, your six-pack belly has turned into six balloons of fat."

Carl was devastated! He quit trying to figure out what had happened and retreated to his bedroom, steaming.

This stage is disorienting. You, as the caregiver, don't know what is going on. Sometimes, there is no defining event, like a fire in the kitchen. Things just slowly get worse. You unknowingly begin to compensate. You begin to decline invitations, using the excuse that you are too tired. Or you blame the kids as they have so many activities, and their homework is difficult. You stop going to the Wednesday night small-group services. You convince yourself that attending church is more than your partner can manage. You had to help your loved one find the chapter and verse the leader wanted everyone to read last week.

Maybe you don't know it, but you are covering and compensating for your loved one's decline. This is a precarious place to be. You know you married a wonderful, talented adult. Or maybe your parent is slipping away. Either way, you are walking through a swamp with no map, no GPS, and no idea where to turn.

Tom knew something was wrong. He didn't know what was wrong, and Terry kept making excuses.

Tom repeatedly took Terry to see the doctor. The excitement and stimulation of going to the doctor's office and talking with the nurses and office staff made Terry perk up, and she was her old, cheerful, gregarious self. While Tom sat in the waiting room, Terry would answer the doctor's questions with half-truths and misleading statements. The doctor said Terry was fine. Tom's frustrations grew at an alarming rate. He knew things were declining, but Terry would throw the doctor's pronouncements of her good health in his face. And the fights continued.

Tom considered getting an apartment or getting a divorce. But he had taken vows, and he kept them. Finally, a neighbor suggested he go into the exam room with her, and during the next visit, he did just that. Tom sat behind Terry, where the doctor could see them both. When Terry said she was fine, Tom would shake his head. The doctor started asking Tom, and he got the chance to explain about the forgetfulness, the loss of day and time, and the need to help Terry dress and shower. Tom insisted on driving her to appointments for her safety. Unfortunately, there was little that the doctor could do. He mostly sent them home with a follow-up appointment in six months. After all, her lab work was fine, her blood pressure medication was working well, her sugar diabetes and A1-C were normal. What did Tom want the doctor to do?

Regrettably, this is a common scenario. Dementia, multiple sclerosis, Parkinson's, and other neurological problems are slow, insidious diseases. There are a few medications that slow the progression in some patients, but there is no cure. Your loved one will die of the complications of dementia. The brain will disintegrate slowly, oh so slowly, until there are not enough neurons to run the body. Then some major organ will fail. It is a slow, nasty death. The authors desire to help you navigate this illness, so you will still have a life, and you can live life with your beloved to the fullest.

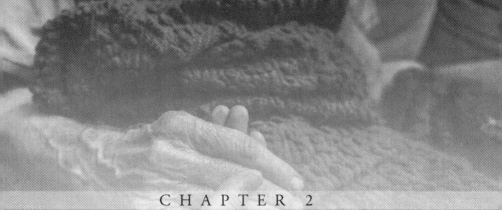

Belligerence Beyond Belief

You and your spouse have been together for many years. You know how they like their meals, how they like to pack for a trip, and how they like to wake up on Saturday morning. You know what they are going to do before they do it. All of this makes your life better, more comfortable, more predictable.

The belligerent stage starts slowly, imperceptibly. Or it may start with an event such as a stroke or a fall. Neither situation is easier or more difficult; they are just different appearances of the same thing. Colloquially, these are two sides of the same coin. It is like the difference between seeing your house from the street or from the air. It is still your house, they are still your spouse, but now things are different.

Perhaps your parents are starting to decline. You may not have a diagnosis yet, but you are starting to wonder what is going on. You may not live with them, but you may be fortunate that you live in the same town. Or you may live several states away. Either way, you may have noticed that they have some problems thinking or even remembering that you called. Their answers have become vague. They are starting to struggle with common activities, like driving. They are beginning to lose the ability to see the consequences of their actions. They may put dinner in the oven and then decide to go play a round of golf, leaving the house with dinner burning. If you and they are fortunate, the entire house doesn't burn down. Either way, you must intervene.

All these problems are grouped into the ugly term "major neurocognitive disorders." This is not a disease by itself. Rather, it is an umbrella term for a group of symptoms caused by damage in the brain. Alzheimer's is the most common form, with about 60 percent of the patients having this diagnosis. Regardless of the medical diagnosis—stroke, Parkinson's, Huntington's, Multiple Sclerosis, Dementia, brain injuries from a stroke, car accidents, concussions, infections, long-term drug, or alcohol use, and so on—the effects will be similar.

As your loved one begins to notice their decline, their frustration increases. For example, they don't want to tell you that they can't remember how to make coffee. So, they unleash their pent-up frustrations on you. For most caregivers, the belligerent stage is the most difficult to manage.

Since you are trusted and available, they take it out on you. Your feelings are hurt, and you don't understand. You want this belligerence, this acting out or this anger, to be a single, unusual incident. You might blame the belligerence on their long day at work or because they didn't sleep well last night. It doesn't occur to you, the caregiver, that this might be something more. You are a trusted, significant person in their life, yet you become the target of their frustration. As the insults and belligerence increase, you pull back. You no longer feel the love, the familiar closeness, the care, or the comfort you expected from this person you love(d). And you certainly don't want to be intimate! Your frustration is understandable. If your parents are declining, the belligerent comments may take you back to your childhood. You may feel like they are lecturing you as though you were a teenager. They don't seem to be aware of all your adult accomplishments. You feel angry and resentful. Regardless, all your feelings are normal.

Then events escalate. Maybe they leave dinner uncooked and retire to the couch with the TV remote. When you come home from a long day at work, dinner isn't ready! Your frustration skyrockets! You are hungry and tired. After all, didn't you get up early to take care of them? When you try to ask about what happened to dinner, they lash out. They ignore your questions about dinner. They change the subject and become even more belligerent. They spew nasty comments like, "I wish you would finally learn what I like!"

The insults and the belligerence continue. The most minor things set it off. You fix his favorite dinner, and your mild-mannered husband starts in about your cooking skills. You take him out for dinner, and all you hear is how bad the food and service have become. You make a special effort to bring the grandchildren over, then he complains about the noise and mess they make.

When people with dementia get an idea stuck in their heads, it stays stuck. Anything you do to try to address their idea will be counterproductive. Generally, the best way to get them to move off an issue is to distract them. The professionals call it "redirection." Don will likely continue to tell everyone that Dorothy doesn't cook anymore. It isn't true, and Dorothy will try to defend herself to her friends. But Don will continue. Dorothy will probably try to give Don examples of the meals she cooks, but it won't help. The only thing Dorothy can do is to agree with Don. She might say, "I really don't have the time or energy to cook lately." Or she might try to distract him, saying, "It's such a lovely day. Let's take a walk."

In the early stages, the caregiver can inadvertently make the belligerence worse. The caregiver believes the loved one is still the brilliant person they once knew. By acting as if the loved one's mind is still intact, the caregiver ends up expecting more than the loved one has the capacity to give. The caregiver believes they are encouraging the loved one, but in reality, this leads to frustration. Because their mental capacity is reduced, the only way the patient can react is by lashing out.

CHAPTER 3

Changes and Caring

With all your frustrations and their belligerence discussed in chapter 2, *you* still have a responsibility. It is up to *you* to care for and help this person who has just insulted and belittled you. *You* are the one—possibly the only—person they can and do count on to get through this latest crisis. Not only that, but *you* may have to give up *your* golf game, *your* time with friends, *your* time at church, and so on because of the demands at home. You may decide it is necessary to find different employment because you are no longer able to travel for work.

These changes may happen slowly. Doctor's appointments are probably the first changes. You should accompany your loved one to doctor's appointments. Many people with dementia are from a different generation, one in which they were taught that you don't complain to the doctor about a pain here or an ache there. Some doctors will probe more deeply, but generally, if there is no physical ailment, the patient is sent home with an appointment for next year.

Marcus took his mom to her regular appointment:

> Marcus said, "I started going to the doctor's appointments with my mom, sitting behind her and shaking my head as she was answering the doctor's questions. The doctor ordered a more thorough lab workup and was then able

to show her that she wasn't doing herself a favor by not
telling the doctor what was really going on."

This puts more burden on *you*. Now you must drive them to the
doctor's office and to the lab. When the lab results come back, there
will be a follow-up appointment. The doctor might add medication,
change the current prescription, or add more frequent appointments.
This will mean more trips to the pharmacy and additional trips to
other therapists or specialists. It will seem like you spend half your time
taking care of them. It never seems to end.

Even though it seems like these appointments are more frequent,
this can be time well spent. If you are helping with the care of your
parent, you can use this time to reflect on your shared past, learn more
about your parent's life before you came along, and reminisce about the
good times. If you are caring for a spouse or partner, you can use this
time to better understand their condition and their needs.

New medication is a double-edged sword. The drug might help, but
it also has the potential for more side effects. Maybe the new medication
will make her dizzy. Maybe your caution about mixing prescriptions
and a few cocktails is ignored. You may need to call the doctor to add
his support to your caution. If they still won't give up their evening
cocktail, maybe you need to hide the car keys at night. Maybe you park
your car behind their car so they can't get out. All these ideas, of course,
involve *you, your* watchfulness, *your* time, and *your* energy.

Selling someone's car and taking away their freedom is a huge
trauma. But if you sell the car this year, it will be worth more. The
decreasing value of the car as it ages makes it worth less every day.
You must also consider the associated costs, including loan payments,
insurance, fuel, and maintenance. All these costs add up at a time
when you may need to conserve finances for the assisted-living facility
or home health nurses. A bigger concern for both the family and the
loved one is the liability in case of an accident. Someone may be severely
injured or worse.

Louis had a series of small fender benders.

Because of a previous medical condition, he was on disability while his wife, Laura, was still working. Laura was beside herself, worried he might hit someone or have a significant accident and be injured. But taking his keys or selling the car meant that he was trapped at home. They lived in a small town without a significant public transportation system. The buses that were available required the rider to step up on the first high step. Louis couldn't manage such a large step. After another accident, the car's tire and axle were damaged, and the car was a total loss. Laura was half relieved that his car was gone but also knew that it would place an additional burden on her shoulders to transport Louis to the doctor, pharmacy, errands, and social events. Ultimately, they comprised, buying him a handicapped scooter. Though it wasn't fast enough to be on the road, it allowed Louis to come and go as he wanted. This took the errands and pharmacy burdens off Laura's shoulders.

Loss of independence brings another series of changes at home. Other conditions, such as generalized weakness, trouble with balance, and uncontrolled diabetes with possible unconsciousness alter domestic equilibrium. Household chores, laundry, cooking, and cutting raw meat or vegetables may become too difficult or unsafe for your loved one. If you are the primary breadwinner and trying to take care of aging parents at the same time, then Pop-Tarts for breakfast and candy bar lunches may be all you can manage, but this probably isn't good for their other health issues. This is where you begin to walk the tightrope of dementia versus diabetes. If it is available in your area, you might want to inquire about a Meals On Wheels provider for lunch. There is a sliding scale based on income, but even at full price, these lunches are reasonable. Generally, the lunch is designed to be more than one person will eat at a meal. The extra food can be saved for tomorrow's breakfast, for dinner with some added vegetables, or used as a midnight snack.

Abby was a gracious, well-dressed hostess and a career woman.

> Alan started to notice that she was not dressing as professionally as she typically did. She always wore jewelry that matched the outfit, but lately she sometimes went without jewelry. Then Alan noticed that she was wearing the same clothing to work two days in a row. Alan had to remind Abby to change clothes every day. She argued, saying the dry cleaning was too expensive.

> Her company sponsored several events over the course of a year. These events were usually to thank larger corporate customers and were quite formal. On the evening of one memorable event, Alan was appalled at Abby's selection of clothing. He took her back to the bedroom and helped her select a different outfit. After some debate, Abby agreed to change. She then selected the jewelry that matched her second outfit. At the event, things went well, leaving Alan to wonder what had happened earlier.

As the disease continues, table manners and other social graces may deteriorate. Your beloved may have trouble using a knife. Instead of cutting the meat, your loved one uses too much pressure, and the steak goes sliding off the plate. Although this seems minor, it may be another indication to you that something is wrong.

Mobility and coordination are other areas where dementia may become noticeable. Perhaps you both loved to dance, but now your partner is reluctant. When you finally get them on the dance floor, your smooth, graceful partner may return. Because of the nature of some dementias, the patients lose their language skills and their ability to walk but retain the ability to sing and dance. Teepa Snow, renowned dementia educator describes this phenomenon using the phrase "Left Language Lost, Right Rhythm Retained."

In the middle to later stages, your loved one may be reluctant to shower and ultimately refuse to bathe. Unknown to you, the noise of the shower or the depth of the water frightens your spouse or parent. The person may have slipped on the wet floor and is now unwilling to step over the side of the tub.

Conversely, your loved one may show more interest or an obsession with household chores. Things such as folding the laundry or emptying the dishwasher may be comforting to him or her. But it confuses you. You don't understand why your partner wants to help in the kitchen but cannot balance a checkbook or plan a meal. This is all new to you.

Social activities, such as going to the grandchildren's soccer games may be wonderful for your beloved. They look forward to the family group and to watching the children play. After the game, there is the trip to the ice-cream parlor. On the other hand, your beloved may balk at going to church. To you, it seems like the same type of family occasion. What you may not realize is that your loved one can't find the page in the hymnal and doesn't remember the words to the song. Rather than tell you about the problem, they would rather tell you they want to watch the football game and don't want to attend church any longer.

The telephone may be another place to watch over your beloved. Many people regardless of age are taken advantage of over the phone. See Chapter 23 for additional thoughts on telephones and dementia patients.

CHAPTER 4

Denial, Dynamics, and Decline

We want the original person back! They are the person we love. They are a part of us. This is the person we grew and changed with. This difficult person cannot be the person we know and love. Yes, it can be. Yes, it is. But as Elizabeth Kübler-Ross wrote in *On Death and Dying*, the first stage is denial.

It is tempting to think an incident is just a phase or single unusual occurrence. If you are reading these words, you may be well past this stage, but perhaps not. And if not, you remember thinking, *"This is odd."* If you had an "event," for instance, a fire in the oven or a diagnosis, it is obvious that something has changed. The problem is that the change is only starting. The dynamics of your relationship will change. You will become the "adult," while your spouse or parent will become increasingly more childlike.

The sooner you understand that what was last week or even yesterday is no more, the more effective you will be at caring for them. Old habits or processes need to change. Giving them up now, quickly, will ease the transition. Both authors fully acknowledge their failing in this area. No one wants to admit something is wrong with their beloved. But every day brings a new set of changes and challenges, and these new situations require fresh solutions and new ways of thinking.

Dave was a contractor who started working at the age of seventeen:

> Dave worked his way up from a laborer, learning to build and fix anything and everything. The boss appreciated his full range of abilities. Many nights Dave would play music for Diane, his wife, and their three girls to start the bedtime routine. He had the gift of music. The piano, guitar, and banjo were extensions of his hands. He played jazz, country, and bluegrass. He made some extra money to support the family by playing in a band on the weekends.

> Eventually, Dave realized he could make more money working for himself, so he started his own contracting company. He was calm by nature and never seemed to get rattled. He was great working with those especially grumpy customers. The company was wildly successful. Dave was always mild mannered; he could work out problems with his customers and his employees. He had a talent for explaining to the craftsmen why he needed something done a particular way and when it had to be finished. His emotional reaction was respectful, social, and business-oriented. He could instinctively interpret other people's expressions, words, and body language. He was a good listener. Dave could get the best out of his workers, and they loved working with him.

> When he and Diane had been married over thirty-seven years, Dave started having problems at work. Eventually, Dave could no longer communicate in a clear, concise, and diplomatic way. Then Diane started to notice subtle communication changes at home. Later, Dave was irritated by every little thing

Diane and his employees did. It got to the point that Diane dreaded Dave coming home as she could feel the tension building.

The complex relationship between husband and wife may be where the first changes are noticed. The husband-wife, husband-husband, wife-wife, parent-child, or significant other relationships are the most reactive. You can politely survive your coworkers until quitting time or look for another job. But leaving your parent, spouse, or significant other is different.

Your parents or spouse know your inner triggers and can push your buttons. They also know by your expressions, movements, and body language when they hit a raw nerve. It is so hard not to react. You don't understand what is happening. You may not know what is changing, but you know you don't like it. You don't know that a disease is stealing your loved one's brain cells.

The brain receives about fifty bits of information per second. The brain is taking in information through the five senses. This information is stored in the computer section of the brain. But as the brain begins to degrade, first the short-term and then the long-term pathways deteriorate.

The connections to ourselves, our spouses, our children, our schools, social life, churches, and old friends don't feel right. Our loved ones may lose the self-regulation and personal limits they once had. Some people may drink more than in the past. Others might take on other unsafe activities, such as climbing on a roof without a harness. These situations become more complex in family businesses because the people involved are more than employees. They are family.

In the early stages, most people are frustrated that their mental acuities are declining. They do not understand how this situation developed, so they react emotionally to people and situations. They may end up in confrontations with their subordinates, their family members, or even a stranger. Then they blame their spouses, bosses, coworkers, or anyone else who is around. It is up to you as the caregiver to recognize these situations and help your beloved.

All people want to be loved and appreciated for who they are, whether in an intimate setting, within their family, or in a business relationship. True unconditional love in any relationship is rare. Most people want to feel and express love, but on their own terms and in their own time. Usually this is when they are ready, in the mood, or feeling good about themselves. As dementia sets in, conditions are seldom positive. Patients still need to feel loved, but often the disease causes them to alienate their loved ones. This is one of the least enjoyable aspects of caring. You must *care*. You must continue to treat them with love and empathy. But this is difficult!

C H A P T E R 5

Exasperation, Exhaustion, and Expiration Dates

You are exhausted and exasperated. The belligerence continues. The insults never stop. The most minor thing sets your loved one off. Eventually, nothing is right.

A person with dementia either doesn't care or is unable to recognize how much effort you are exerting on their behalf. They don't care or are unable to recognize that you have had a long, stressful day at work. They don't care or are unaware that you have a challenging career and demanding boss. You are tired. Your home used to be a sanctuary; now it is a battleground. You are frustrated, angry, annoyed, and infuriated. And worst of all, there is no support system for you, nothing to help you decompress or help you recharge. You want to throw yourself on the couch with the TV remote and hide. It is easy to forget that the adult you knew isn't there mentally anymore.

Emily shared,

> Ed and I were struggling. I was still working. Ed was
> fired after his breakdown at work. This prompted the
> trip to the doctor and the diagnosis.

Last week, when Ed's sister dropped in to visit, I was swamped at work and so tired. I bought a premade dinner from the store. That set Ed off. He began to rant, "This isn't good enough, I want Chinese." So, I ordered Chinese to be delivered for the three of us. But Ed's complaints continued. He started a tirade, telling his sister, "Emily could have made ten meals for the price of this junk!" I was shocked, hurt, angry, and embarrassed. I tried to explain to my sister-in-law, but Ed was on a roll, berating me to her.

I excused myself to get out of the room and let them talk. I was so embarrassed that I wanted jump off a bridge. Then the hurt turned into tears while I hid in my room. I can't complain about an ill spouse; I'll sound like the grumpy old troll Ed makes me out to be. And I know my sister-in-law will repeat the hateful things Ed said. She will spread the rumors like wildfire. She always makes me the bad guy!

Emily used to be rock solid. She related with others diplomatically and could conduct herself with grace in all circumstances. Now she is being ground down like a rock that has fine sand blown over it. It feels like a wind is carrying away all the small pieces of her composure and some of her personality. She used to be a mountain of strength. Now she feels half as strong as she once was. Emily almost doesn't recognize herself anymore.

Nor does her boss care that she has problems at home. He doesn't care about all the extra work Ed requires, exhausting her. The boss still expects her to meet the production schedule with professionalism, to be on time to work, and to put in a little extra overtime taking care of everything he needs. He expects Emily to do everything with grace and style. He says, "After all, that's what I pay you for."

Emily continued,

> Ed's doctor ordered more lab work, and this will place
> another burden on me. Now I must decide whether to
> let drive Ed himself to the lab or if I should take more
> time off work. I know that when the lab results come
> back, there will be a follow-up doctor's appointment.
> The doctor will want to add a new medication or
> increase the current dose. Either way, this means more
> appointments. This means more trips to the pharmacy
> to pick up the new medicines, more appointments,
> more work that I will miss. My boss will not be
> happy with me. And that new medication the doctor
> suggested has nausea as a common side effect. If Ed
> gets nauseated, he might fall rushing to the bathroom.

It! Never! Ends!

Emily had lunch with her friend and discussed,

> Should I use my already depleted sick leave to take Ed
> to the lab or save it to hear what the doctor might have
> to say? Should I risk letting Ed drive to the lab? Ed
> told me at dinner that he drove to get coffee with the
> guys. But that was yesterday. How is Ed doing today?
> How about tomorrow when he has the blood draw? I
> know he has good days and bad days. But lately he is
> having more bad days than good days.

None of this is new to you. All these decisions involve *you*, *your*
watchfulness, *your* time, *your* energy. And they all sap your strength,
exhausting you. Exhausted as you are, you can't sleep. You lay your
head down but your mind goes over and over all the nuances, all the
behaviors, all the changes. You wonder, *what is next? What is yet to
come?* How are you going to manage the next step? Can you retire

to be their full-time nurse and survive financially? What about your group health insurance? If you quit work to care for your loved one, your group health insurance will likely disappear. What if neither of you is old enough for Medicare? If you quit, there won't be any health insurance. So no, you can't quit. Your loved one needs more care. But you are close to being vested in your own retirement and could retire in a few more years. You'd never be able to work twenty years at another company. If you quit now, will you have enough money to survive when you retire? Over and over, your mind churns with options, strategies, and choices. By morning, you are exhausted and have no more clarity than last night. And you still must get up and go to work for that boss who is pushing you for higher quotas.

If only Emily knew exactly when Ed would need to stop driving, the exact day! And the day he would need to go to adult day care, and exactly when he would need twenty-four-hour inpatient care. But alas, none of us is born with an expiration date. If Emily knew the answer to any of these questions, she could make hard and fast decisions. Emily might have the clarity to wait to take her Social Security when she was seventy and not retire until she was fully vested so that she would get the maximum retirement check to establish her own future. Or she would know to retire early, take Social Security at sixty-two, and take care of Ed. But without that exact date, she will have to muddle along, making the best decisions she can with incomplete information. You will be in the same place, making critical decisions without enough information, all while you are too exhausted to think clearly.

How do you know you're exhausted? It starts early in your day; the alarm clock goes off, and you sleep through the first couple rings. You want to stay in bed, pull the covers over your head, and avoid the day. Then when you do get up, your eyes are tired and scratchy. You know it's not pollen. It's just that your eyes haven't been open long enough. You force yourself out of bed and head for the bathroom. You stand in the shower with your eyes closed and think about what to make Ed for breakfast. You know Ed will want bacon and eggs. Not again! You don't want to cook bacon and clean up the splatters. Hopefully, he'll settle for instant grits. You are so tired. The water feels so good! Then you realize what time it is. You don't have time to wash and curl your hair and make breakfast too. Your hair will have to wait until tomorrow. Ed comes first!

When you are this exhausted, your body can't make you less tired. If your body needs more oxygen, it will automatically breathe faster. But your body can make you find a different source of energy … food. The doughnuts someone brought to work will call to you all morning. And the birthday cake with all the sugary frosting might keep you going in the afternoon. When you get home, you still must fix dinner, start laundry, do the dishes, and clean up. Then, your beloved wants you to watch a TV program with him. When you fall asleep on couch, he gets upset and storms off to the bedroom. You slip back into that wonderful comforting sleep.

Emily continued,

> I heard a noise and woke up, startled. It's 2:00 a.m. Ed is in the bathroom, and there is a huge mess. Unfortunately, I'm still dressed from work, in my suit. Should I launch in and clean up the poop now, before Ed smears it all over? I'm still in my dress clothes! If I go upstairs to change, will Ed come with me rather than attempt to clean up, making it worse? Do I change into jeans or my pj's to start cleaning? Will I need a second set of pajamas before I get everything back in order?

There is no right or wrong answer. Emily just must wing it. All these tasks and decisions lead to exhaustion. When your personal hygiene starts to take a back seat to chores, you are exhausted. When you start turning to junk food for extra energy, you are exhausted. When you drag yourself through your day and then drag yourself through chores at home, you are exhausted. When you find yourself sleeping in your clothes, you are more than exhausted.

This situation is past the point where Emily needs help. Emily will not be able to help Ed if she falls asleep while driving and has an accident. Or if she is in a drowsy fog and walks into traffic. Or if her blood pressure gets high, leading to a stroke. Recognize your exhaustion before there are long-term consequences. All these things happen to caregivers every day. You think these things won't happen to you. But they might. These are signs you need additional help. Do *not* damage yourself while taking care of the patient. You are the most valuable resource your loved one has, and if you are unwell, you can't be an advocate for his or her needs.

This is the point where a change in thinking is required. Money becomes less important than your health. At this point, you must outsource some of the chores: transportation, meal preparation, hygiene, and so on. You must save your energy to be their advocate.

Yes, finances will be tight. Ed can't work. You, like Emily, are probably the breadwinner now. Hiring someone to sit with Ed will make finances tighter. Possibly your church can help. Maybe your town has an adult day care. But Ed doesn't think he needs help. He says he is perfectly fine and asks why you are such a worrywart. Yet another fight ensues. What are you going to do?

If neither of you is old enough for Medicare, Medicaid may be an option. Medicaid is a program for low-income families. Like any other government program, transitioning to Medicaid is complicated. You may need the services of a Medicaid consultant.

Watch out for these signs you are exhausted and approaching caregiver burnout:

- You feel increased irritation, frustration, or anger over trivial things.
- Your gentle, unhurried approach to providing care is disappearing or gone.
- You raise your voice at your loved one more often and later feel upset and guilty.
- You often skip aspects of your loved one's care that are important to their well-being because they're just too difficult.

- Your mental health is declining; you may be struggling with increased anxiety, depression, or insomnia.
- Your physical health is declining. Perhaps you've had to increase medications, or you have injured yourself while trying to transfer your loved one.
- The demands of care for your loved one are harming your family.

At this point, *you* are the most valuable resource your loved one has. *You* must protect *your* health, your finances, and most important, your sanity.

CHAPTER 6

Family, Friends, and Flying Blind

Including quantum physics in a book about caregiving may seem strange. However, in a real sense, it applies here. The renowned physicist Dr. Stephen Hawking proposed that there is not one history of everything in the universe; there are infinite histories. In his theory, particles may take any of the infinite paths, each with its own probability of occurrence. These pathways vary in probability from the extremely high (walking directly to a neighbor's home) to the infinitesimal (going to a neighbor's home by way of an island in the South Pacific Ocean). While any of these is possible, only one path can be taken.

The same philosophy can be applied to caring for a person with dementia. Every option is available, but only one can be selected. You must select the best path to take. There will be positives and negatives with any decision you make. Family and friends will be the source of greatest help and greatest hindrance as you navigate the ever-changing landscape of caring for someone with dementia.

For this discussion, we assume you have the of Power Of Attorney for your beloved. If so, know that:

- *You* are in charge. Decisions about the direction of care and what you do are yours and yours alone. Other people—including friends, family, and acquaintances will second-guess you. They will snipe to others about the way you are managing things. These comments will get back to you. Do your best not to let it bother you. Just know it will happen. Know that as long as you make a decision with love and empathy, it is the right decision.

- This is *your* situation. No one else—no friend, no family, not even the multitude of doctors you will encounter on this journey—will know everything you know and do. No one else will have all the facts, all the history. And no one knows what will happen in the future. You will need to make decisions based on incomplete or incorrect information. Be aware of how extremely uncomfortable this will be. You will second-guess yourself. Be kind to yourself. Allow yourself to be human and forgive yourself for any errors you may have made or will make.

- Friends and family will offer incredible amounts of advice. While well-intentioned, none of your friends and family have the ultimate responsibility *you* have. They will criticize you for the decisions you make and the actions you take. There is nothing you can do about this. Any attempt to change these people will be as effective as attempting to stop the sun from rising tomorrow. You must continually remind yourself that *you* are in charge. The course of action you decide to take is yours and yours alone. While others may snipe, no one can completely understand your situation. By extension, none of them is qualified to pass judgment on you.

It is critical that you know family members will separate themselves into a few broad categories. Even worse, they can move between these categories at will. These categories are the Peacocks, the Parrots, the Vultures, and the Seagulls.

The first group we call the Peacocks. They will be happy to preen around you telling you what they have been doing and the last vacation they took. They will sprinkle in old platitudes and how they could never do what you are doing. They will waste your time asking about how you are and pumping you for information about your loved one. They do all this to show off to their friends. They want to be the first to say something over the proverbial backyard gossip fence, otherwise known as social media. They want to be the center of attention while they spill the details of your life to everyone. The best way to deal with the Peacocks is to not give details. Say simple things like, "He is holding his own," "He is about the same," or, "The doctor was encouraging at the last visit." Another favorite is, "She has good days and bad days." If they press you for your condition say, "I'm doing fine." or, "It is busy at work." The authors have found it is best to change the subject and ask about the Peacock's family: "How is your mom? I heard she was sick." Peacocks want to preen and show off their feathers but don't offer any assistance.

The second group is Parrots. They want to squawk and show how important they are. Or worse, they will tell you how bad their recent cough and cold was and how sick they were. They want to squawk misplaced advice and suggestions. They want to be a hero by helping you with nothing but empty advice that they have heard somewhere else. When the Parrots give advice, they automatically feel superior and elevated in stature because they feel they are smarter than you. They may be goofy as can be and their advice may be contrary to your experience, but they will continue talking and suggesting until your head is ready to explode. While they probably won't say this outright, this will be the message you get from them. "Get on with your life." Other advice and assistance can be in the form of, "Put him in a home, and move away." (Placement situations are examined in more detail in chapter 14.) Thank them for the advice. Then say something like, "I will consider that," or, "That is an interesting idea." Remember, you don't need to follow or consider any of their suggestions. When the Parrot flies away, things get quiet again, and you can breathe.

The third group is the Vultures. They might be the distant cousin who just wants all the photo albums because of their interest in family genealogy. Of course, you want the photo albums. They are yours and contain all your memories. These are the memories of the good times, the fun trips, and the children as they were growing up. Soon, the photos may be all you have left. Rather than lose your cool and bluntly telling your cousin "No," say, "Maybe later." Or, "I've already promised them to someone else."

Other Vultures may circle the deathbed either in reality or from afar. They have their eyes on something a little further in the future. They may view you as the obstacle to an inheritance or advise you to get a divorce. After all, they are waiting for Daddy/Mommy or Uncle/Aunt Grandma/Grandpa to pass away so they get their share of the estate. If you are gone from the family, their share might be larger. Vultures can be counted on to help only themselves. Don't count on a Vulture to help with any of the hard work.

George lived in a different state than his family.

> He was out making the final arrangements for his mom's funeral and wondering how to be the executor of the estate. When he got back from the funeral home, he made coffee. He went to the cupboard and found every coffee cup, every glass, every lamp, and pieces of furniture covered with sticky notes. His siblings labeled the entire house and split up all their mom's things. George's name wasn't on a single item!

> His legal counsel told George to remind his siblings that they could ask for things, but he was the executor and had her medical bills and legal bills to pay. Most of Mom's valuables would have to be sold to settle her debts. His brothers and sisters were furious at George. George had to bury his mother that week, and he really didn't need the family conflict on top of

everything else. Eventually, his mom's house did have to be sold, and George tried to honor the sticky note avalanche. As he packed up, he wondered where his siblings were. They certainly were not there to help him with the hard work.

The fourth group are the Seagulls. They are loud, messy, and arrogant. They fly in, dump on everything you have done, diminish any trust you built with the other members of the family, and then fly away. They provide nothing in the way of real assistance. They make lots of noise and get in the way of caring for your beloved. They are relatives or friends who rarely come to visit and do so at inconvenient times. They seem to have an opinion on everything associated with your loved one's condition and jump to incorrect conclusions.

Franny, Frank, and Fred grew up in a small town. The family encouraged education, sports, and ethical behavior. Their parents went to all the soccer games, the school plays, and the PTA meetings.

Franny always wanted to be a fashion designer. She wanted out of the small town, so she moved to New York City, where she quickly climbed the corporate ladder. Franny loved the city with the plays, restaurants, and the sophisticated life. On the other hand, Frank and Fred went to college, returned to their hometown as professionals, and started their own families.

As their parents aged, the boys began to take care of the parents. It started out simply with mowing the grass or shoveling snow after a storm. As the years passed, more and more care was required. The guys took time off work to drive their parents to doctor's appointments and made trips to the pharmacy to pick up medicine. Their wives helped with keeping the house clean and doing the grocery shopping.

Things were stressful, but the four adults juggled their own families and careers while taking excellent care of their parents. When Dad fell, the brothers felt that Franny was needed at home to assist with decisions concerning him. Possibly he needed expensive inpatient care. Maybe they could get some help in the home. But what would Mom need? Could she stay in the family home alone? What if she fell? Would she have enough money to pay for care for Dad and provide a reasonable quality of living for herself?

Franny agreed to fly home. She arrived Friday night, visited with her parents briefly, and went to her hotel room, saying she was tired from the travel. Saturday, a family dinner was planned with the three generations. Grandma and Grandpa had a wonderful time reminiscing about when their children were small. Franny made some snide comments about the furniture being old-fashioned and that the TV was too small. She also commented that their parents' family car needed to be replaced. It wasn't new enough.

Franny took some family photos and then announced that she had plane tickets for the next morning. She was working on Monday and wanted to have time to herself to rest before her commute in New York City traffic.

Frank and Fred were shocked. They had planned to have this exceedingly difficult discussion at Sunday brunch. Instead, they called Franny out to the patio, where it was quiet. The brothers started to tell Franny about the difficulties with their parents' situation including finances and health. But Franny didn't want to hear it. She pronounced, "They look pretty good to me." She left for her hotel room soon after and returned to the city the next morning.

After a meeting with the medical staff, it was decided to move Dad to a nursing home. They called to tell Franny about the decision. She exploded but offered no constructive suggestions. She didn't think Dad needed that much care and was appalled at the monthly cost. She wondered how much would be left in the estate.

Franny is a typical Seagull. She wants to be involved only in the fun parts of life. She made it quite clear to her brothers that the parents' home was not stylish. Through her comments, she let it be known that she wasn't interested in small-town problems. She was going back to her sophisticated life. She would not even discuss her parents' issues, let alone any workable solutions. And she certainly wasn't going to provide any financial support.

Dealing with Seagulls is the same as dealing with Peacocks: Nod your head and encourage them to leave as quickly as possible. Frank and Fred should ensure that they have the Power Of Attorney and other legal documents so they can make the best possible decisions for their parents' care. Then when there is a significant change in health requiring a move to a facility, Franny should be notified. She should be told that the facility is expensive, and the cost will decrease any estate money she might have been planning on. Franny will, of course, complain. Seagulls by nature squawk, scream, and protest.

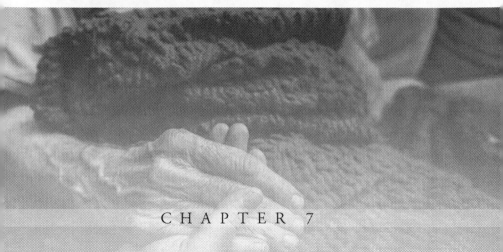

CHAPTER 7

Guilt, Remorse, and Forgiveness

Guilt is assigning blame to oneself for inadequacy or moral failings. Guilt descends on us when we believe, correctly or not, that we have been inadequate, broken a moral code, or caused harm to another. Remorse is the regret we feel for committing this breach or inadequacy. Guilt focuses on the one who committed the transgression; remorse focuses on the person who was wronged. As a caregiver, you have plenty of opportunities to experience both, often over the same incident.

Everyone is human. Everyone has shortcomings and inadequacies. You are likely not a trained caregiver, and you have had to learn caregiving on the fly. You will make mistakes; you will have to take shortcuts or stretch the truth just to get through the day. This is not a breach of any moral code or a sign of any inadequacy. If you have done your best to care for your loved one with dignity and love, you have no reason to feel guilt or remorse. Forgive yourself!

As much as you will obsess over your loved one's care or worry about what you have done right or wrong, your beloved will complain about what you are doing *to* them. Meanwhile, your loved one will ignore everything you have done *for* them. You will be accused of all sorts of imagined transgressions. These accusations and complaints will create feelings of guilt on your part. Your beloved cannot see the downside of you not taking care of them. All your loved one knows is that life now is not the one they had before this debilitating condition entered their life. They won't recognize the decline, and you will bear the brunt and blame for the perceived changes in your beloved's life.

Just because you have no reason to feel guilt or remorse does not mean these emotions won't wash over you like rain. Guilt is that overpowering heavy feeling or cold empty feeling in your chest that comes over you after you hurt someone. Remorse is the result of that pain in your heart, telling you that you should apologize. In some ways, it is worse than embarrassment. You may have hurt your beloved's feelings, but did they have to tell the whole town? Why didn't they tell the rest of the story? But when you do apologize, the feelings don't stop.

Because of anosognosia (being unaware of one's medical condition), they may not even be aware they are failing. Due to this same lack of awareness, your loved one will probably lash out, criticize, and berate you for an imagined mistreatment. And those comments, coming from someone you love, will be like a knife in your heart. They will wait unit the optimum moment to figuratively grab that knife and twist it. Your beloved will tell half-truths, imaginary complaints, and outright lies to the pastor, the doctor, the neighbors, and other family members. You will feel shame, anger, and worst of all, guilt. The insults will take their toll. You may wish your beloved was gone. When you recognize this, the guilt will come back stronger than ever. You will wonder how you could ever wish that. Forgive yourself. These feelings are a side effect of the guilt.

As long as you are the adult in the room, you have no reason to feel guilt or remorse. Of course, just because you have no reason to feel the emotions doesn't mean you won't feel them. Everyone struggles with emotions. You are doing your best to take care of your beloved and move forward. Don't take that blame. It is not yours. Admit that you do not have the patience of Mother Theresa. Occasionally give in to their whims and let them have what they want. Make life easier on yourself. Keep treating them with love and dignity. Trust yourself that you are doing your best.

Commonly, your loved one will insist that they are fine. And as mentioned previously, they will not even be aware they are failing. Your beloved will insist that they can still drive. You, as the husband/wife, son/daughter, will see them driving thirty miles an hour on the freeway, causing a hazard. You will also make sure that you both attend church on Sunday morning. In order to keep them off the road at night you will say that the Wednesday night service just isn't what it used to be and offer to stay for an in-home bible study or family game night. The Wednesday night service fiblet will leave you feeling guilty for lying. You should justify it as protecting others who won't get hit by the car. But that drop of guilt will persist.

Think about your situation from a societal perspective. It is estimated that Alzheimer's and other dementias will cost the U.S. health care system more than $259 billion in 2017, with costs potentially increasing to $1.1 trillion by 2050. There is hope that even modest progress in treating Alzheimer's disease can drastically change this trajectory. If a new medicine could delay the onset of Alzheimer's disease by five years, roughly $367 billion annually in long-term care and other health care costs could be avoided by 2050.

(https://www.phrma.org/-/media/Project/PhRMA/PhRMA-Org/ PhRMA-Org/PDF/MID-Reports/MID-Alz-Update_FINAL.pdf)

These costs are medical expenses, but there are other societal costs. Because the patients are unable to recognize their diminished capacity (anosognosia), they are statistically at greater risk for accidents or criminal acts (commonly hitting, headbutting, shouting, screaming, swearing, scratching) that may lead to an arrest. Or there may be violence toward the nurses or caregivers, causing the facility to discharge them and requiring you to move them to another facility. As a caregiver, you need to be more proactive, moving your loved one to a higher level of care before they become violent. When they become violent, the facility must protect the other residents. If this happens, the facility may find it necessary to discharge your beloved. You want control the situation and keep the facility from making this decision. Your beloved will want to go home and will assure everyone they can manage living in their apartment or house. After all, they may have been getting physical therapy and are stronger than when they came in. In truth, it is the diminished mental ability, not physical ability, keeping them in the facility. They are not able to manage paying the bills, maintain the home, care for themselves, maintain a schedule, call for help, or keep the home hygienic. The logic becomes inescapably circular. Because of diminished capacity, they are unaware of their diminished capacity. Your beloved will swear that you are mean to them, and *you* are the problem. Don't accept the guilt or remorse. You are doing your best.

To avoid feelings of guilt, remind yourself that it is the disease causing the behavior, not your beloved. Yes, it will look and sound like the person you love, but the person you knew is leaving a little bit at a time.

Guilt is a heavy burden to carry, and you are likely already tired and worn to a frazzle. Your beloved incorrectly feels that you are doing something bad to them. You are not! Don't take on the guilt that your loved one wants you to carry.

One method to stop the guilt from building is to know that these challenging behaviors are cyclic. First is the trigger. You have no way of knowing that they have decided to have cookies for breakfast. Then the issue escalates. No matter how kindly or lovingly you explain that you have made this lovely breakfast just for them, and they need the protein, they still want cookies.

Gus and Gretta are a typical story,

> Gus was trying to feed Gretta the correct amount of protein to control her diabetes, just as the doctor and dietician told him. Gretta perceived it as Gus making her eat a yucky breakfast of bacon and eggs. Gretta wanted cookies!
>
> When the eggs were done, Gus put the bacon and toast on a plate. As he carried the plate to the table, his formerly calm, rational, loving wife continued to insist on cookies. Gus kept walking to the dining

room, hoping the old habits of sitting at the table and eating together would take over. But his sweetheart purposely hit the plate, sending food everywhere.

At that point, Gus was in crisis. Gus really wanted to take a swing at his wife, punching her right in the mouth. But being the adult in the room, Gus controlled himself. But he still wanted to punch her in the face!

When Gus realized this, the guilt welled up in his chest. How could he want to punch this wonderful woman? He wondered, *What makes me feel this way? I love this woman. I married her, she gave me three wonderful children, we made a life together, and now I want to punch her until she shuts up. What is wrong with me?*

The guilt is overwhelming. Gus should notice that his beloved is not listening to anything rational. She wants cookies. Gus knows cookies are not good for her sugar level but identifying the trigger—in this case cookies—may assist Gus to avoid escalating and then moving into crisis mode. Maybe he could give her cookies instead of the toast. Possibly handing her one cookie while he finishes cooking will help. The trick is to avoid escalation. In other words, stop the fight early. This will help you to avoid carrying more guilt.

Gus continued,

This morning was a struggle over the cookies, but the rest of the day went well. I made dinner and then Gretta said she would clean up. She started the dishwasher, wiped down the counters, and defrosted something for tomorrow's dinner. It was wonderful! Just like years ago. But then I felt more guilt! How could I have underestimated her? What else had I done to demean her? Things are going to be fine. The doctors were wrong. I've heard of so many incorrect diagnoses on TV. This happens all the time. This is such a relief. Things are so pleasant tonight, just like years ago. I went to bed and slept all night. A deep, restful, restorative sleep. I slept just like our babies. It was wonderful. That is until the next morning, when I got up. I couldn't find Gretta. I looked in every room. Finally, I raced outside and saw her wandering a block away in her bare feet and nightgown. I grabbed my shoes and brought her back home.

When Gus decided that the doctors were wrong, he fell into denial and found that denial is a wonderful place to be. There is hope and comfort in the "Land of Denial," but unfortunately, you can't live there. Not being awake and allowing your spouse to wander may increase your guilt. This is guilt that you really shouldn't be carrying. The dementia made Gretta wander, not Gus. Gus needed that sleep.

The dementia won't get better. Things will be worse tomorrow and probably the day after. You want your adult loved one back, but that person is gone for good. So be kind to yourself. Accept that you don't have the patience of the biblical Job. Occasionally give in to your beloved's whims and let them eat the whole carton of cookies. Make life easier on yourself. Trust yourself and do what must be done. Prioritize the most important things, and let the other things go.

CHAPTER 8

Hang On

As stated previously, you may start down the dementia path due to an event, or you may start with a series of minor changes. Regardless of how you start, you are in for the ride of your life. It will be easy to fall into the "Caregivers' Rut." A wise man once said, "A rut is just a grave with open ends." You know you are in the Caregivers' Rut when every day becomes like the day before and the next day too. Days, weeks, and months look like an endless stream of the same thing. It is important to recognize this and begin to plan for it. There will be endless laundry, doctor's appointments, spills to clean, and carpets to wipe. There will also be hurt feelings.

Just like on a roller coaster, there will be ups (good days) and downs (bad days). There will be unexpected twists and turns (diagnoses, falls, and trips to the emergency department). Going up is always slower than coming down. That is, the good days don't seem to be as good as the bad days are bad. The situation is constantly changing. Sometimes the change is imperceptible, but things are always changing.

You will know you are deep in the Caregivers' Rut when your old friends don't call anymore. You have turned them down once too often. Perhaps your loved one was too difficult to deal with, ruining the fun of the evening with friends. Try not to let this happen. You deserve a girl's night out or a poker game with the guys. Get your daughter, son, or best friend to come sit one evening, so you can go out. If your family is a long distance away, consider respite care. Yes, these services have a cost, but this cost must be balanced by your need for a break. The thing to remember is this: Don't kill yourself keeping them alive.

When someone says, "Call me if you need anything," stop them right then and there and reply, "That's so kind. I really want to see that new movie. Could you come over on Tuesday night?" Don't let that opportunity slide by; take them up on the help immediately. Maybe you need a sprinkler head replaced, the lawn mowed, or a drippy faucet fixed. Tell everyone what you need. Don't be the martyr who does it all yourself. You need the break. The break will help you help your beloved. You will be a better caregiver when you are rested and refreshed.

Without reaching out for help, caregivers often exhaust themselves. Worse than exhaustion is when caregivers pass away before their beloved. It is commonly thought that premature death of the caregiver is due to not paying attention to their own health.

Helen was doing the finances for her elderly parents and taking care of her beloved husband, Hugh who had vascular dementia caused by a stroke.

One day Helen took Hugh to their family doctor. The doctor examined him, ordered some medication changes, and then asked them to remain in the exam room. The nurse came in with a chart not for Hugh but for Helen. The nurse took her temperature, blood pressure and weight, and drew a sample of her blood. Shortly, the doctor came back into the exam room. He explained to Helen that her blood pressure was in the stroke range, and he would like to call an ambulance to take her to the emergency department for IV drugs. Helen would not leave Hugh, and she was skeptical about the doctor's alarm. Helen and the doctor compromised. The doctor gave her some samples of blood pressure medicine and watched while she swallowed them. After monitoring Helen for an hour, her blood pressure was coming down, and her lab results were back. Helen's blood sugar was high, her cholesterol was high, and her weight was high. Helen agreed that her fitness level had to be corrected. The doctor reminded Helen that she wouldn't be available to take care of the family if she continued down this path.

Helen and Hugh went home. While fixing dinner, she realized that something had to change. She called their priest, and he agreed to come to the house. After discussing Helen's situation with her, the priest suggested that Helen attend the rosary meditation on Tuesday nights. The priest was also able to find someone to sit with Hugh while she was gone. Helen found the rosary meditation helpful and decided that she could sleep in on Saturday. On Sundays, Helen got Hugh up and dressed, and they both went to Mass. Hugh enjoyed staying for coffee and donuts. He was calmer on Sunday afternoons.

Helen found some other people in the church who were caregivers for their own loved ones. With her spiritual needs met and the creation of a support system of new friends, Helen also found some peace.

CHAPTER 9

Indicators

Chances are that when you look back, you will recognize many indicators that you did not see when they first presented themselves. The problem is that the early signs are subtle. It is tempting to dismiss them as a bad day, fatigue, or apathy.

In Ila's case, she was an elegant woman. Her home was immaculate, her hobby was entertaining her friends with elegant dinners, themed parties, and intellectual discussions.

After her diagnosis, there were signs from three years earlier. At one of her dinner parties, she arrived looking like the most elegant homeless person. Everyone figured she was only tired from preparing for the party and dismissed it as an anomaly.

Another time she forgot what time it was and didn't get the meat into the oven. The beef didn't have time to cook fully. Her guest (and best friend) saw the dilemma, cut some slices, and placed them into the microwave before the other guests noticed.

A few months later, she celebrated her birthday in her pajamas with her entire extended family around her. Again, everyone figured she was tired from the merriment of her birthday. Her teenaged nieces, however, thought she was wearing the latest fashions.

As Goldfinger said to Bond, "Once is happenstance, twice is coincidence, the third time, it's enemy action." In the case of dementia, thrice can be the earliest sign you get that your loved one needs help. Thrice is time to make that doctor's appointment. It is also time to begin researching long-term care and respite facilities available in your area.

Before the diagnosis, your beloved probably had borderline unspecified dementia. This is where problem-solving and attention loss (shifting to other subjects) become more pronounced. It is also where judgment and abstraction difficulties begin. Some patients experience verbal and memory problems. All this is aggravated because the patient has decreased awareness of their challenges.

Ivan's wife started to notice that things were different at home,

> His retail business suffered because he could no longer keep his inventory correct, complete necessary government paperwork, or even make appropriate changes due to the economic climate. However, he covered for these symptoms by having his employees manage those details. Soon after this occurred, his wife noticed the change in the store's profitability. She asked the employees and found that the paperwork was indeed not completed as she would have expected.

Ivan had trouble with the paperwork and inventory, but why? *Was he not aware it was the end of the quarter and time to do inventory?* Semantic clues are a gentle way to help your loved one remember duties and schedules. You may want to start a conversation with, "Remember when we took inventory at the old store? Well, it's time to take inventory again." Semantic clues may make your life easier and help anchor your loved one in time and space.

Dementia Indicators

Dementia is not a specific disease but a general term. Although dementia generally is found in the elderly, it is not considered part of normal aging. Dementia is the impaired ability to think, make rational decisions, and behave in a normal manner. Dementia generally causes difficulty in remembering common things—such as one's address—making simple decisions, completing tasks alone, or other problems that interfere with everyday activities. Dementia's symptoms can vary widely from person to person. But in general, people with dementia have problems remembering things, maintaining attention (ability to focus on a task), reasoning, and problem-solving.

Dementia is considered a collection of symptoms and is not diagnosed unless there is impairment of at least two brain functions, such as memory loss and judgment. Medications and therapies may help manage symptoms for some patients. As of this writing, there is no cure for dementia in any of its forms. Being tired and forgetting you left your keys on the counter is not dementia. Forgetting what the keys are for ... that is dementia.

The strongest known risk factor for dementia is increasing age; most cases affect those sixty-five years and older. A family history of dementia also increases the chances of dementia. Race and ethnicity increase the odds of getting dementia. Older African Americans are twice as likely to have dementia than Whites. Hispanics are one and a half times more likely to have dementia than Whites. As of this writing, the cause for these demographic differences is not known. If left untreated, poor heart health, including high blood pressure, high cholesterol, and smoking, increases the risk of vascular dementia. Head injuries, including strokes, can increase the risk of dementia, especially if the injuries are severe or occur repeatedly.

A health-care provider will order tests on attention, memory, critical thinking skills, and other cognitive abilities to see if there is cause for concern. A physical exam, blood tests, and brain scans, such as a CT or MRI, can help to determine if there is a treatable underlying cause.

People who demonstrate dementia-like symptoms may have a reversible underlying cause such as side effects of medication, increased pressure in the brain, vitamin deficiency, or thyroid hormone imbalance.

After the doctor has given you a diagnosis, the medical community will need a reference point called a baseline. The baseline will be used to measure decline from the original point at diagnosis. Because dementia has no cure at this time, the patient will continue to decline, though there are some medications that may slow the progression. Each medication is only effective for a limited number of diagnoses and a limited number of patients. Not all medications are effective for a given person. If your loved one stabilizes, then the medications will tend to delay the progression of their dementia.

One example of baseline testing will be to determine if your beloved can group items together. This is called abstractions, or the ability to group things or concepts into categories. For example, if the doctor asks the patient how a banana and an orange are related, the patient may not be able to group them into the category of fruit. It is common for the patient to try to distract the doctor by talking about the orange tree they had as a child or how wonderful the oranges tasted, rather than answer the question.

Physical Health Indicators

The most accurate predictor of dementia health is physical health. If the patient gets a cold, flu, urinary tract infection, or other physical problem, the dementia symptoms are likely to worsen. The good news is that after the patient recovers from the temporary physical problem, the dementia is likely to return to the level it was before the illness occurred.

Exercise can slow the progression of dementia, so try to persuade your loved one to exercise. Exercise will increase aerobic fitness and help to prevent falls. Additionally, a diet rich in vegetables and proteins will keep them well nourished. Many elderly people are unaware of their hydration levels. Attempts to encourage adequate water intake will assist with general health and may prevent urinary tract infections. You may also want to ask the doctor to recommend a daily vitamin that will work well with their current prescriptions.

Overview of Dementia Types

There are several types of dementia. Different types of dementia present quite differently. Common symptoms include forgetfulness, limited social skills, and compromised thinking abilities. Everyone has forgetful periods, but dementia is persistent and exceeds normal limits.

- *Alzheimer's*
  Alzheimer's is the most common form of dementia. Alzheimer's disease is a type of brain disease, just as coronary artery disease is a type of heart disease. It is caused by damage to nerve cells (neurons) in the brain. Testing can eliminate some other causes, but Alzheimer's disease can't be diagnosed with 100 percent accuracy until after an individual dies and a neuropathologist performs an autopsy.
      Symptoms that may indicate Alzheimer's disease include:

  - Memory loss
  - Problems with planning or problem solving
  - Losing track of time
  - Misplacing things
  - Poor decision-making
  - Problems with speaking or writing
  - Changes in mood and personality

- *Vascular Dementia*
  Strokes and resulting brain damage are the second most common form of dementia. Some patients have other issues regarding blood flow to the brain. Diabetes, high blood pressure, and high cholesterol are known risk factors. Symptoms vary depending on the area and size of the brain impacted. Some patients will

be paralyzed on one side of the body, while others may have mild confusion. As the disease progresses, the patient may take a large step down and then be stable for a period.

Symptoms may suddenly get worse as the individual experiences more major strokes or ministrokes called transient ischemic attacks (TIAs). Typically, symptoms of vascular dementia include the following:

○ Slowed thoughts or impaired ability to make decisions, plan, or organize
○ Reduced emotional response
○ Difficulty with motor functions, especially slow gait, and poor balance

• *Frontotemporal Dementia (FTD)*
FTD can be extremely difficult to diagnose accurately because symptoms vary strongly from person to person and are like other forms of dementia. Some patients have memory loss, while others may get lost in their neighborhoods. Three main groups of symptoms exist for the disease, all stemming from the degeneration of the frontal and temporal lobes of the brain.

As the disease progresses, FTD patients tend to exhibit a notable difference in behavior. This can include the onset of lethargy and a lack of spontaneity. Other people exhibit complete disappearance of inhibitions. In other patients, social withdrawal appearing as depression is common; some patients opt to stay in bed all day. Patients with FTD can sometimes engage in inappropriate behaviors, such as sexually charged verbiage or in a few cases, criminal activity. Though rare, some patients also experience psychotic symptoms such as delusions, paranoia, and hallucinations.

Typical early symptoms include marked changes in personality and behavior and/or difficulty with producing or comprehending language. Unlike Alzheimer's, memory is typically spared in the early stages of the disease.

- *Hydrocephalus*
  A condition characterized by excess fluid buildup in the cavities of the brain, hydrocephalus results in physical and intellectual impairments. In certain stroke patients, the brain cavities may fill with blood, causing excess pressure in the brain. Red blood cells cause irritation and death of the brain cells. If any of the following symptoms are noted, take your loved one to the emergency department:

  o Chronic headache
  o Nausea
  o Difficulty in focusing the eyes
  o Difficulty walking or changes in gait
  o Weakness in legs, falling
  o Drowsiness
  o Changes in personality and behavior, for example, irritability
  o Seizures

- *Lewy Body Dementia (LBD or DLB)*
  Not every patient with LBD will experience every sign and symptom of this form of dementia. Regardless, sudden or severely shifting changes in behavior or cognitive functioning should be reported to a doctor. Common symptoms of LBD include:

  o Slow, rigid movements
  o Shaking
  o Balance issues, falling
  o Fainting
  o Difficulty with concentration and alertness
  o Visual hallucinations
  o Daytime drowsiness
  o Fluctuating changes in personality or mood
  o Memory loss
  o Confusion
  o Problems sleeping

- *Progressive Nonfluent Aphasia (PNFA)*
  Family members notice a gradual decline of verbal fluency. Patients begin to struggle with speaking (articulation) and are unable to make the appropriate sounds, demonstrating increased phonological errors. They may make syntactical errors in common speech, such as mixing singular and plural in the same sentence. One notable difference from other forms of dementia is that PNFA patients typically retain word comprehension and understand what others are saying. PNFA is why your beloved can't always find the word they want and struggle to find another word as a substitute.

- *Semantic Dementia*
  The opposite of PNFA, the patient with semantic dementia speaks in complete, rational sentences (semantic dementia preserves syntactic fluency), but they cannot comprehend what others are saying.

Falling

Another indicator of dementia is loss of balance resulting in falling. Patients may fall if they are tired, ill, or just because of random events. If your loved one falls and is heavier than you, larger than you, or unable to assist you in getting up, immediately call 911! Many fire departments will be happy to send a rescue team to pick up your beloved and set them in their favorite chair. An additional benefit is most teams have paramedic skills and can assess if your loved one needs to be seen at the emergency department. This additional level of attention will comfort you. The authors suggest that more than two falls in two months is an indication that your beloved has progressed to the moderate stage of dementia.

Incontinence

Both men and women may suffer from incontinence. Stress incontinence is commonly identified by the leaking of small amounts of urine when exercising, coughing, sneezing, laughing, or lifting. The leaking is due to the urethral sphincter being unable to tighten completely. Pelvic floor exercises (Kegel exercises) may help.

Leaking of large amounts of urine without enough warning to get to the bathroom is urge incontinence. It is also known as having an overactive bladder. The cause may be spontaneous relaxing and then returning to normal contraction of the detrusor muscle.

In women, as hormones decrease after menopause, the urethra may weaken, leading to incontinence. Women may suffer from both stress incontinence and urge incontinence. Women who have symptoms from both types are said to have mixed urinary incontinence. Mixed incontinence is most commonly caused by age, but pregnancy, childbirth, and obesity may also lead to incontinence by weakening pelvic support structures.

Men, like women, may also suffer from an overactive bladder, leaking large quantities of urine. They can also suffer from stress incontinence. This most commonly happens after prostate surgery and/or radiation therapy. As with women, the sphincter cannot clamp down completely. This allows small quantities of urine to leak out of the urinary bladder during activities such as coughing, sneezing, or laughing.

Older men often suffer from an enlarged prostate, causing a bladder hindrance. The prostate surrounds the urethra, and the lower lobe grows throughout a man's life. This increasing size squeezes the urethra, making emptying the bladder more difficult. Behavior therapy of going to the bathroom on a regular two-hour schedule (during the day) may assist in reducing the urgency and help to manage accidents.

Regardless of sex, age increases problems with incontinence for everyone. Other diseases such as diabetes, multiple sclerosis, prostate cancer, or stroke can cause or aggravate incontinence.

Urinary Tract Infection (UTI)

UTIs are common in both men and women and should be treated immediately and aggressively. A UTI may lead to an increase in incontinence in both men and women. Some patients will be unable to control the urine flow and suddenly find themselves with wet clothing. Other patients will delay urinating as the infection will produce a burning sensation and pain. Aggravating factors are obesity, constipation, smoking, and caffeine intake. Caffeine is found in coffee and soft drinks and is a mild diuretic, causing mild dehydration. To help combat UTIs, encourage your beloved to drink at least thirty-two ounces of water or other non-caffeinated beverages every day.

If your beloved's behavior takes a radical shift, have them checked for a UTI. Because of the lack of control of bladder and bowels, elderly people with dementia are more susceptible to UTIs.

UTIs are serious. They can spread throughout the body. The most common way to tell if your loved one has a UTI is if they are belligerent, not in their "right" mind," or refuse to go to the bathroom. You will wonder what is going on with the first UTI, but after that, you will know to be watchful for the signs.

Double Incontinence: Becoming a Member of the Blue Glove Club

Double incontinence is also known as urinary/fecal incontinence. It is due to weakness in the same muscle group as the bladder. While it is not easy for a caregiver to deal with urinary incontinence, poop is a whole different ball game. Fecal matter is sticky, stinky, and more acidic. This acid can break down the skin and lead to other problems. Poop smells bad and stains the sheets, the carpets, and the chairs. It's hard to get an adult, especially an overweight adult, to twist and turn so that you can get them clean, really clean! Sometimes it is just easier to get your loved one into the shower. But no matter how you approach this accident, it's a mess! You want to be as calm as Mother Theresa, but the smell, the mess, and your embarrassment are difficult to cope with. You didn't sign up for this! You remember the competent parent or the adult you married, and that person is gone! What you have in front of you is a belligerent, embarrassed, angry, smelly person you don't recognize. You are unbelievable sad. You don't want to do this. None of this! You want to go on a cruise and be catered to, have drinks poured for you, and to lie under an umbrella in the sun. Since that isn't possible, you want to go to your room, pull the covers over your head, and hide. The bathroom accident is emotionally devastating for you. Although both of you will suffer when bathroom habits change, for you, it is another sign of the decline and finality of your beloved's disease.

Meanwhile, your loved one is embarrassed and distressed. They will try to hide the accident and try to clean themselves. This usually increases the mess and makes actual cleanup more difficult. If your beloved is in the belligerent stage, they will aggravate the cleanup process. Your beloved will argue with you and tell you they are fine, that they can clean themselves, or that you are not doing a "good enough" job. This type of reaction cancels any type of rational discussion. An effective way to manage this is accident is to say soothing things, like, "It happens to everyone." If these words gag you and stick in your throat, you are normal. These words may not be true, but soothing statements tend to calm the situation. So, grab some blue gloves, clean up your loved one, and try to hide the tears.

In any case, the health of the skin is paramount. Adult diapers may keep the skin drier and healthier. If you can transition your loved one to adult diapers, your life will be easier, and your laundry will decrease. But if your loved one is embarrassed and belligerent, a rational discussion of adult diapers will likely not be possible. You might try replacing the cloth underwear in the dresser drawer with paper underwear. If you are lucky, they will wear the paper underwear.

CHAPTER 10

Jargon and Terms

Abstractions

Making abstractions is the ability to pull things or concepts from something broader and group them into categories. For example, if the doctor asks the patient how cows and sheep are related, the patient may not be able to group them into the category of animals. The patient may try to distract the doctor by bringing up a vacation taken as a child and how exciting it was to see the cows in the fields.

Activities of Daily Living (ADLs)

https://findanyanswer.com/what-are-the-5-activities-of-daily-living

ADLs are a series of basic activities necessary for independent living at home or in the community. There are variations of the definition of the ADLs, but most organizations agree there are five basic tasks:

Personal hygiene	Capability to bathe or shower independently, perform personal grooming, nail care, and oral care.
Dressing	Ability to make appropriate clothing decisions and the ability to physically dress and undress oneself.

Eating	Ability to feed oneself, though not necessarily the capability to prepare food.
Continence	Awareness of the need to use the restroom and physically get to a restroom. This includes the ability to get on and off the toilet and clean oneself.
Transferring/Mobility	Ability to stand from a sitting position, as well as get into and out of bed. The ability to walk independently from one location to another.

Alzheimer's Disease

https://www.mayoclinic.org/diseases-conditions/dementia/symptoms-causes/

As mentioned earlier in this book, Alzheimer's disease is the most common cause of dementia. Although not all causes of Alzheimer's disease are known, experts do know that a small percentage are related to mutations of three genes, which can be passed from parent to child. While several genes are probably involved in Alzheimer's disease, an important gene that increases risk is apolipoprotein E4 (APOE).

People with Alzheimer's disease have plaques and tangles in their brains. Plaques are clumps of a protein called beta-amyloid; tangles are fibrous and made up of tau protein. It is thought that these clumps damage healthy neurons and the fibers connecting them.

Anger

https://www.idrlabs.com/anger/test.php

It may seem obvious when your loved one is angry. What you might not realize is that anger can be broken into dimensions. Psychologist Judith Siegel's Multidimensional Anger Inventory (MAI), developed in 1986, including the Multidimensional Anger Test, evaluates those dimensions:

- Anger Arousal: Frequency, magnitude, and duration of angry responses.
- Anger Spectrum: The range of situations likely to trigger an angry response.
- Hostile Outlook: How cynically/suspiciously one views the world.
- External Anger: The tendency to take anger out on external surroundings, including other individuals.
- Internal Anger: The tendency to internalize anger and/or not share it openly.

  o *Anger Arousal*
  As one becomes angry, the body's muscles tense up. Inside the brain, neurotransmitter chemicals known as catecholamines are released, causing bursts of energy lasting several minutes. The frequency, magnitude, and duration of anger-causing activities will increase in the middle stages of dementia.

  o *Anger Spectrum*
  Frustration and angry feelings, feelings of nervousness and upset feelings can range from mild annoyance to yelling, breaking objects, and ultimately hurting people or pets.

  o *Hostile Outlook*
  Dementia patients often develop a suspicious worldview. They frequently have fears of break-ins, thefts, and criminal activities. They are sure that the cars driving down the street are watching them. These worries often lead to feelings of anger and fear. Hostile feelings can morph from worries about people breaking into the house to hostile feelings about their spouses and caregivers.

○ *External Anger*

External anger is the tendency to take anger out on people or things external to themselves. Usually, this begins with complaints, such as being critical of your cooking, how you are dressed, or the TV programs you like. The criticism may escalate to yelling, arm waving, and mimicking punching you. The patient probably feels rage, high levels of tension, and threatened. The next stage of anger is breaking objects, typically in the house. This may lead to injuring the family pet or worse, physically assaulting the caregiver.

○ *Internal Anger*

Anger is an intense emotion felt when something unfair has happened. Everyone feels anger occasionally, but caregivers are especially prone to internalize their anger and not share it openly. The caregiver will stuff their angry feelings because they know that their beloved is unable to cope, that it wasn't their fault. Internalized anger is typically accompanied by feelings of stress, frustration, irritation, and increased fatigue. These factors can lead to worsening physical conditions such as increased blood pressure.

Aggravating the situation is the fact that the loved one's verbal attacks may seem to come out of nowhere. The criticisms are generally out of proportion to the situation. Later in the disease, the beloved may escalate into physical attacks. Commonly, the caregiver makes excuses to protect their loved one. Even though the caregiver knows full well that the bruise on their leg was because their beloved hit them with the cane, the caregiver will ignore or make excuses for the action. This same type of silent abuse is found with abused wives in houses without a dementia patient. These sudden and possibly catastrophic reactions to a seemingly normal situation are often triggered by necessary care.

Anosognosia

A condition or symptom that causes a patient to be unaware of their status, for example, when a person is strangely unaware of having a broken leg. Someone with anosognosia who has a broken leg might sign up to run a marathon. But the caregiver knows the leg is broken, sees the cast or the boot, and empathizes with the groan of pain when they put pressure on the leg but will be unable to convince the patient of the condition.

Aphasia, Progressive Non Fluent (PNFA)

https://www.mayoclinic.org/diseases-conditions/dementia/symptoms-causes

This is a gradual degrading of verbal fluency (the ability to speak) where patients begin to struggle with articulation (forming words) and make syntactical (grammar) errors. Generally, patients retain their comprehension (understanding). This causes frustration on the part of the patient and possible misunderstanding on the part of the caregiver.

Assessment before Acceptance

Assisted-living facilities, including those with memory care, and nursing homes are not allowed to accept someone whose needs are too great for the residence. An assessment is required before moving into assisted-living or other facilities to determine what type of care is necessary and whether the facility can provide it.

Assisted Living Facility (ALF or AL)

Assisted Living residences combine room and board with medical and personal care. They are often suitable for someone in the early stages of Alzheimer's disease or related dementia. Services offered in assisted living include meals, help with activities of daily living (ADLs), social activities, and transportation to and from doctor's appointments. Before moving in, the facility will assess your loved one to confirm a good fit between the facility and your loved one. See: "Assessment before Acceptance." Full-time supervision means residents are safe and receive the prescribed medication and nutrition.

The living units may be studio apartments or have one or two bedrooms. Someone with mild to moderate dementia can still feel a sense of independence. For instance, the family can take them out of the facility to lunch or to church.

The family will need to furnish the apartment. This is a mixed blessing as the patient will be surrounded by their familiar furnishings. But the family will have the chore of moving the furnishings both into and out of the facility when the patient leaves.

Baseline

The status of the individual when first diagnosed. The baseline is used to measure decline from that point onward. Because dementia currently has no cure, your loved one will continue to decline. As mentioned earlier, there are a few medications that slow the decline, but they are only effective for some diagnoses and some patients. But if the medications are effective for your loved one, the medications delay the progress of the dementia.

Borderline Unspecified Dementia
https://www.agingcare.com

This is beginning stage of dementia, where problems become noticeable. Problem-solving and attention shifting (lack of focus) become more pronounced. Difficulties with judgment and abstraction begin. Some individuals experience verbal and memory problems. Aggravating this is that individuals lack awareness of their challenges.

Burnout of Caregivers

https://www.verywellhealth.com/signs-of-caregiver-burnout-97981

"Seven signs of burnout:

- You feel increased irritation, frustration, or anger over trivial things.
- Your gentle, unhurried approach to providing care is disappearing or gone.
- You raise your voice at your loved one more often. Later, you feel upset and guilty.
- You often skip aspects of your loved one's care that are important to his or her well-being because they're too difficult.
- Your own mental health is declining; perhaps you're struggling with increased anxiety, depression, or insomnia.
- Your own physical health is declining. For example, you've had to increase your high blood pressure medication, or you've injured yourself when trying to transfer your loved one into a wheelchair.
- Your own family is experiencing dysfunction, and your care for your loved one is harming your family."

Delayed Recall

Delayed recall is a predictor of dementia's progress. A common test is to give the individual a list of words to remember. The tester will explain that they will be asked to repeat the words in fifteen minutes. If the person can't remember any of the words, they are at the end of the moderate stage and entering the severe stage.

Delirium

https://www.cdc.gov/aging/dementia/index.html

When experiencing delirium, the individual sees or hears things that don't exist. They may be restless due to perceived threats, or they may drum their fingers on the arm of the chair to the rhythm of music only they hear. They may speak incoherently, as if they have a strange new language. The caregiver may think they are dreaming and or are only half awake. This is a severe sign.

Dementia

As mentioned elsewhere, dementia is not a specific disease but a group of mental conditions that interfere with the tasks of daily living. Generally, dementia is not diagnosed unless at least two brain functions are impaired, such as memory and judgment. Medications and therapies may help manage symptoms. Common symptoms include forgetfulness, limited social skills and thinking abilities, possible hallucinations, lack of balance, and inability to take care of bodily functions. In everyday language, everyone has forgetful periods, but being tired and forgetting the keys is not dementia. Forgetting what the keys are for may be an indicator one has dementia.

Dementia Care, the Cost of

https://www.phrma.org/-/media/Project/PhRMA/PhRMA-Org/ PhRMA-Org/PDF/MID-Reports/MID-Alz-Update_FINAL.pdf

Alzheimer's and other dementias will cost the U.S. health care system more than $259 billion in 2017, with costs potentially increasing to $1.1 trillion by 2050. There is hope that even modest progress in treating Alzheimer's disease can drastically change this trajectory. If a new medicine could delay the onset of Alzheimer's disease by five years, roughly $367 billion annually in long-term care and other health care costs could be avoided by 2050.

Denial

https://www.psychologytoday.com/us/basics/denial

Denial is a defense mechanism where an individual refuses to recognize or acknowledge objective facts or experiences. This is an unconscious process that protects the person from the situation.

Hallucinations

Individuals with dementia may experience perceptions of stimuli that don't exist. For example, seeing a locomotive in the house or hearing music that is not playing. The caregiver may notice that the individual may be restless, pacing, or is drumming his or her fingers on the arm of the chair. These outward signs may give the caregiver clues to investigate further the patient's mental state. See: "Delirium."

Hospice

A hospice is a facility that offers end-of-life care focused on comfort and palliative care, not treatment.

Illusions

Unlike hallucinations that are imagined, illusions are real stimuli that are misinterpreted. A typical example is a dark mat in front of a door misinterpreted as a hole in the floor.

Memory-Care Facilities

Memory-care facilities are specifically designed to deal with issues related to dementia. Staff of these facilities are trained to communicate with the residents who have reduced cognitive abilities, to watch for depression symptoms such as withdrawal, and to encourage individuals to socialize and participate in activities.

Mild Cognitive Impairment (MCI)

A condition in which people have memory or other thinking problems greater than normal for their age and education, but their symptoms are not as severe as those seen in people with dementia.

Nurses, RN, LPN, VPN

RNs are registered nurses or nurses with more education and certifications than other nursing levels. LPNs are licensed practical nurses, and VPNs are vocational practical nurses who are able to dispense medications and observe the patients' conditions. Jointly, these nurses provide and manage most of the medical care. Nurses dispense drugs, conduct some procedures (such as starting an IV), and manage schedules for doctor appointments, allow other technicians to draw blood, take X-rays, etc. They can be considered the foremen of the medical industry.

Nurses' Aides or Certified Nursing Assistants (CNA)

These are the worker bees of the medical industry. They are the ones providing most of the direct care for your loved one. These people are responsible for providing individual comfort and taking care of his or her hygiene.

Nursing, Director of (DON)

Also called a charge nurse, he or she supervises other nursing staff, audits medications, and watches over patient progress.

Parrots

These friends and family offer well-meaning but misplaced advice. Commonly, the advice will range from being useless to damaging or detrimental. Don't feel the need to follow the advice but say soothing things to encourage them to leave.

Peacocks

Seemingly cheerful people who want to know how things are so they can inappropriately gossip about your loved one to others. Try to distract them with questions about themselves or their family.

Primary Care Provider (PCP)

This person is the individual's main physician, nurse practitioner, or physician assistant.

Rules of Caregiving

"One, it will be difficult. Two, it will be worth it" (Laura Finney). "Although your loved one may not remember you or might do things that frustrate you, this is the time when he or she needs you the most" (Angie Nunez Merryman).

Seagulls

These are friends and family members who fly in from far away for short periods of time. While they are with you, they criticize everything you say and do. Seagulls cause problems by diminishing the trust you have built with the patient, then they fly back to their lives. They leave you to pick up the pieces of your relationship with the patient.

Semantic Clues

Semantic (verbal) clues can be used to help your loved one remember things. They may make the caregiver's life easier as the clues will help to anchor your loved one in time and space. For example, "Remember when we took that trip in 2005? That's when we bought the new car." Or, "The doctor wants to see you again. Tomorrow, we will have to get up and get dressed so that we can see the doctor."

Showtiming

Someone with dementia can be witty and charming for a brief time, such as at a doctor's appointment. They are showing their capabilities for a short time. This behavior will exhaust the patient. After resting, the individual will return to their previous dementia level.

Sundowning

Sundowning is a neurological phenomenon associated with increased confusion and restlessness in people with delirium or some form of dementia; it is most commonly associated with Alzheimer's disease. Sundowning seems to occur more frequently during the middle stages of Alzheimer's disease and mixed dementia and seems to subside with the progression of the person's dementia.

Despite its name, sundowning is not necessarily caused by the change in light levels, though that may play a factor. Sundowning is likely to occur due to a disruption in the circadian rhythm—that is, the body's clock—of people with dementia. This can cause them to have disruptions in their sleep patterns. As the day wears on, the person with dementia becomes more tired and is therefore more likely to be confused and agitated.

If your beloved is awake and upset:

- Approach them in a calm manner.
- Find out if there is something they need.
- Gently remind them of the time.
- Avoid arguing.
- Offer reassurance that everything is all right.
- Don't use physical restraint. Allow them to pace back and forth as needed, with supervision.
- Attempt to distract them or redirect their thought patterns.

Urinary Tract Infections (UTIs)

Urinary tract infections are common in men and women. UTIs should be treated immediately and aggressively. Infections of any type will exacerbate dementia symptoms. Individuals with dementia are particularly susceptible to UTIs due to incontinence. When a loved one's behavior changes significantly and quickly, they should probably be checked for a UTI.

Vultures

Friends and family who want possessions or money are referred to as Vultures. They will not help with the patient or the patient's care, but they will be there to collect their share of the estate when the patient passes away.

CHAPTER 11

Kindness Concerning Hospice

At some point, you have likely considered that your loved one will leave you and cross over into heaven. You may have considered the complications and freedoms after they cross over. Having the professionals discuss hospice with you is no small matter. You will never forget the discussion of moving your loved one to hospice.

When doctors and nurses approach you about hospice and begin discussing it as the "next step," it will sound like *hospice!* You will experience conflicting emotions; the first one is guilt. At this point in the journey, you will be familiar with that cold, empty feeling of guilt—guilt that you could not do more for your beloved, that you may have missed something, that you didn't get help soon enough, and so on. That cold, empty feeling in the pit of your stomach is familiar. You have already replayed every decision you made along this journey, and you will again and again, continually questioning yourself and wondering if you could have done something different or better. As we said in the Introduction, if you are reading these words, be kind to yourself, you did your best, and you have our respect.

The second emotion you will feel, making the guilt worse, is relief. Perhaps this nightmare will end someday, and you can get your life back. At this point you are tired and tired of being tired. You have watched this person you love deteriorate to nearly nothing.

The purpose of a hospital is to treat patients, returning them to health. The purpose of hospice is comfort care, not treatment. In some places, hospice is run by a larger medical facility, though there are some stand-alone hospice facilities.

Hospice care maybe provided in the home with the assistance of the professional staff. Many patients desire to die at home. Assisting a loved one to die at home is a major undertaking for the family. Families need to understand that hospice care for someone with dementia is a lengthy process as many patients survive six months or longer. Unlike cancer or other diseases that can be tracked by CAT scan or an MRI, dementia deterioration is difficult to predict.

Patients may beg to be taken home; home is where they are most peaceful. However, the family may already be exhausted from caring for their loved one. Does the spouse or primary caregiver have enough physical or emotional reserves to provide attentive, loving, dignified care for the individual? Can the family provide the physical care for someone who is bedridden? Can the family provide the correct diet? Can the family physically turn the loved one to clean them after a bowel movement? Does the family know how to change sheets while the loved one is still in bed?

As death nears, new medications may become necessary. Pain medications are a common need. The patient may develop other new symptoms. High fevers are common. The patient may develop terminal anxiety or seizures that can be helped with medications. Breathing difficulties called Cheyne-Stokes respirations may start, with long lapses in breathing followed by fast gasping breaths.

Another respiratory issue is colloquially called the "death rattle." As the patient receives pain medications that induce sedation, respiration may become depressed. The lungs then have problems clearing excess fluid. This happens with any cold, flu, or other respiratory illnesses. However, with pain medications, the coughing instinct is reduced or diminished, making the patient unable to clear the fluid.

Breathing difficulties are challenging for the family to observe. The emotional toll on the family is immeasurable. The caregiver and the family will begin the grief process, called anticipatory grief. They will have tears, anger over past problems, and fears of what the future will be like without their beloved.

In-patient hospice care in a facility is not inexpensive. There is generally an entrance fee with daily fees twice those of a luxury hotel. Room and board fees at the hospice facility are usually considered maintenance costs and are ineligible under Medicare and most health insurance plans. Insurance will generally pay for professional services such as doctor's visits or for nurses to administer medication.

Home hospice is less expensive than a medical facility as room and board are provided by the family. But there is a price to be paid for saving this money. Nurses and nurse's aides are not immediately accessible for the patient's needs or to assist with the family's emotional support. When your beloved is on hospice protocol, you will no longer dial 911. You will be provided with a dedicated number to call when you have questions or needs. For the same reason, when your beloved passes away, you will not call 911. In hospice, death is not an emergency. But be assured, this, too, will be managed with as much dignity and respect as you would wish.

With in-home hospice, physical maintenance of the individual becomes the family's responsibility. This includes keeping the loved one clean, turning the individual at regular intervals, providing the necessary food and medication, bathing, and other maintenance chores. If you are the primary caregiver, think about your willingness and ability to do all this before you select home hospice. Other family members will vote for home hospice and say things such as, "Dad would want to be at home. He told me he wants to go home." They will sometimes even say they will help with Dad's care. This is *not* the time to believe family members who haven't helped in the past will suddenly step up and help. (See Chapter 6, Family, Friends, and Flying Blind.)

If you are helping with making this decision, consider everything that has happened. Is the family, especially the primary caregiver, physically strong enough, and do they have sufficient stamina to do the physical work of nursing? Are they emotionally strong enough to handle sitting by the bedside and allowing the dying process to take place? Will the caregiver change their mind and want the doctors to intervene? The physical and emotional needs of the caregiver must be considered.

Beyond the conflicting demands of the patient, family conflict, and anticipatory grief, there is one other issue to consider before deciding to provide hospice care at home. That is, when you get ready to sell the family home, how do you answer the potential buyer's question, "Has anyone ever died in this house?" While this may not be a reason to avoid home hospice, it is one more thing to consider when making the decision about whether to provide hospice care at home or in a facility.

Regardless of where hospice occurs, there are two things that will strike you about hospice. They both involve caring. Up to this point, you have wondered why it is called health "care" as no one seems to care. The people at hospice are the most kind and caring you will find in your journey. The other thing you will notice is a lack of urgency. If your beloved develops a fever, it won't be treated with medication. Instead, a cool washcloth for the forehead will likely be provided. In our experience, blood pressure will be taken only once, at admission. From that point on, the purpose of the staff is to keep your loved one comfortable, not to treat their ailment.

CHAPTER 12

Living Your Life Is Not Losing Theirs: The Placement Decision

The most valuable resource for someone with dementia is their caregiver and the support system. This system should include doctors, nurses, family members, other paid care support staff, neighbors, friends, etc. Additionally, internet message boards can be a source of practical information and an outlet for venting when things are difficult. Caregiver burnout is a real issue with this disease. It is easy to become overwhelmed with demands, requests, needs, desires, and guilt.

As stated previously, *you* are your loved one's most valuable resource. You cannot do this alone. This bears repeating. *You cannot do this alone.* If you try to go it alone, you run a significant risk of diminishing your effectiveness and your health before your loved one dies. To be an effective advocate, you must maintain yourself. This includes physically, mentally, and emotionally. Dementia will take a toll on you. There is no way that it cannot.

Physically

You must maintain yourself physically. This includes a proper diet, an exercise routine, and relaxation. Beyond your physical body, though, you need to keep your physical environment maintained. This includes your home and its support systems, the furnace, the water heater, the sewer, and so on. These must all be maintained in working order. If these systems fail, your caregiving efforts will be significantly compromised. Your transportation system must be well maintained. Keeping a person with Alzheimer's distracted while changing a flat tire in the rain requires infinitely more effort than changing a tire in pleasant weather. Find a good mechanic and keep him or her aware of your challenges.

Mentally

You will be stressed tremendously. You will question yourself, your decisions, your motives, and your actions. You will need a support system to help you through this journey. This may be one or two family members or a small number of your current friends. You may find that friends and family become as scarce as hen's teeth when you need help or a sounding board.

Emotionally and Spiritually

This process will suck your soul dry, and there is nothing you can do about it. Therefore, you need a support system. You need people in your life to whom you can turn to recharge your batteries. A close friend or your church or spiritual adviser may help you to manage this time of your life.

You will see the person you love decline. Then you will watch them decline further. And when you think they cannot sink anymore, you will watch your loved one decline again. Then you will have to watch the process again and again. There is nothing you can do about the decline. Eventually you will lose your loved one. At times, you will resent that they are still alive. Near the end, you will hope—and occasionally pray—that the suffering for both of you is over soon.

You will be frustrated beyond belief. The brilliant, articulate, funny adult you knew has slowly been replaced by a belligerent, ignorant, incontinent, two-hundred-pound child. You will wonder what you did to deserve this. There is nothing you can do about it. This is a game your beloved will lose, and you will lose your loved one.

Although it may be cliché to say, "It takes a village" to care for a person with dementia, it is true. As in the army, the bullets to beans ratio (the number of people required to support one frontline soldier) is about 12:1. While the ratio in the dementia fight may be different, the concept is the same. In this fight, you are on the front line, so you must have a support system.

Eventually, caregiving for someone at home may no longer be appropriate or feasible. Either the needs of your beloved will become overwhelming, or you will become exhausted. It will be time to move your loved one into a twenty-four-hour care facility with trained staff. There will be no other choice about moving your beloved to a facility. You won't want to, but you will have to accept the situation. This will not be giving up on your loved one. You have already determined to love them until the end. But you must find the strength to do what needs to be done, what is best for your beloved. This process is extraordinarily traumatic. The guilt will beat you up with unanswerable questions and unresolvable issues. Accept this. Forgive yourself. Your victory will be having your health intact at the end of this journey. Because there will be no other victory, there is no virtue in losing your life in this fight.

Discussions on proper placement should be had with the doctor and other professionals. Depending on your beloved's condition, options may include independent living (IL), assisted-living facility (ALF), adult day care (ADC), and memory care (MC). Each of these services has its advantages, problems, and associated costs. You, however, are the one who must decide which option to select. You may become trapped by your desire to keep the person you know as close as possible. Don't wait until this happens to begin the process of placing your loved one in a facility. Placing your beloved in a facility is not as easy as making a hotel reservation or an online purchase. There are many steps, and many people are involved. Each one can derail the process. If you are reading this chapter, it is time to begin considering the placement decision. The question of when to call for help or to place your loved one in a facility is a balancing act. Your desire will be to delay bringing in help until the last possible moment. There are many reasons for this. It is heart-wrenching and disruptive. You also know that a care facility is expensive. When you place your loved one in a facility, you will feel like you have failed. However, the consequences of not having help when it is needed could be real failure. Your loved one may fall and break a bone or wander off and not be able to find their way home. More significantly, you may become a victim of burnout or injure yourself caring for your family member. If either of these occur, you will not be dealing with the guilt of feeling like a failure. Rather, you will be dealing with the consequences of failure itself.

After you place your beloved in a facility, you must transition from caring for them to managing their care. Instead of direct contact with your beloved, you work through your support system of doctors, nurses, and other support staff. But you remain the hub all these people revolve around.

Some Assisted Living Facilities (ALFs) offer "memory care units," "special care units", or "Alzheimer's care units." A memory care unit is better suited for someone in the middle stages of dementia when independence has become difficult or impossible. Memory care may be a wing or special section of an ALF, or a dedicated stand-alone memory care home. Dedicated homes are more appropriate for people in the moderate to severe stages because their staff is specially trained to communicate with and care for people with dementia. Speaking with someone who has dementia requires a specialized technique. Similarly, activities are carefully planned for people with dementia and are more considerate of their abilities to participate, function, and understand.

Memory care facilities have physical designs appropriate for people with dementia. For instance, a person with Alzheimer's may become upset when encountering a wall, so these facilities often have hallways without sharp corners; they are designed in a circle. Because people with dementia are prone to wander, memory care facilities have increased security and supervision and special locks on the doors.

The question becomes: *When should you move your loved one to a long-term care facility?* There is no clear answer. This is not as easy as making a reservation at a hotel for a vacation. You need a facility that is both a good fit for your beloved, and just as important, has a vacancy, in parlance, an available bed.

You may have delayed making this decision, and now your beloved has become violent or hospitalized due to an injury. You are now trapped by the system. You will have to deal with hospital discharge planners and social workers. You will be confused, bewildered, and afraid. The staff will impart a sense of urgency. Hospitals are not a permanent placement. Your beloved must go home or to a facility. Simultaneously, the discharge planner will appear to be rushing you to make a decision while at the same dragging their feet rather than providing the assistance you need. The discharge planner may not be allowed to assist you in choosing a facility. Depending on your location, the planner's ability to help may be limited to giving you a list of local facilities. If you are fortunate, the list will include some that specialize in caring for dementia patients. You may find what is called a continuous care facility with a mix of patients. Your beloved will be included in a mix of Assisted Living, Memory Care, and Physical Rehabilitation facilities for people recovering from things like knee or hip replacements. If you are in a rural area or small town, the nearest facility with a vacancy may be miles away.

When you ask about these things, the social worker or discharge planner may gloss over your questions and concerns. They may employ guilt, double talk, and misdirection. They may omit vital details, all while exaggerating some and minimizing other crucial elements. Their job is to move your loved one out as fast as possible. They will want you to believe that they are kind, empathetic, and attempting to assist you, while in fact, they are trying to get your beloved out as soon as possible.

Medicare will only reimburse the hospital for a certain number of days, and your loved one's days there are numbered. As soon as Medicare says they must go, one of two things will happen. Either you start paying the hospital from your own resources, or your beloved goes home. This is not the time to learn that you do not have your beloved's Power of Attorney. (See Chapter 14, Navigating the System.)

With panic in your heart, you begin to call all the facilities on the discharge planner's list. The admissions clerk, community-relations manager, or someone with a similar title tell you that they will have to conduct an assessment of your loved one. They will ask for records and other paperwork. It will sound simple enough, but it will quickly become complex. First, you must call the hospital to find out how to release your beloved's private medical information to an outsider. You will eventually be transferred to patient records, where the staff will explain that you must sign a records release for each individual facility being considered. In some cases, this can be completed electronically; in other cases, you must go there in person and sign the form. If it is summer in Florida, and you were going to visit your loved one this afternoon, it will all work out easily. However, if Florida is having a hurricane and the roads are washed out, you will be delayed. The discharge planner will be calling you and telling you that your loved one is going to be discharged now! Come and get your family member now! Tick, tick, tick.

In your best, calm, rational voice, explain to the discharge planner that you are working with the ABC facility, and the ABC staff will be contacting the hospital soon. You can request the discharge planner to call the ABC facility directly. But always make soothing noises to calm the discharge planner and get him or her to hang up.

But now you are upset, so you call your neighbor Lee (a peacock.) Lee listens to your story and promptly tells you how awful the ABC facility is. Lee's wife, neighbor, or parent had a terrible experience at the ABC facility. When you hang up with Lee, you feel even worse than you did before the call.

You need to start looking at other facilities. You remember the social worker mentioned that Medicare.gov has a rating system. You dive into the Medicare search box and enter "ratings." But now what? There are so many, and the clock is still ticking. You call a few facilities that are closer to home. You talk to the community relations manager or other admissions person. They need medical records. But there is the hurricane and flooded roads out there. They don't have an electronic signature system. Now you must wait. And wait. But you know the discharge planner will be calling soon. Tick, tick, tick.

Tick, tick, tick. You are stressed tremendously. You question your decisions, your motives, and your actions. You want your formerly adult loved one back. You begin to think you could just bring them home. You believe your beloved would be fine. Yet intellectually, you know better. Besides, the professionals know best, and they want your beloved in a facility.

Tick, tick, tick. You have a few facilities in your area and have picked your favorite. You feel a major sense of relief. You go in to sign the paperwork and find out the last bed was taken that morning.

Again, your stress level increases. You question yourself again. How could you not ask about availability? Your decision process must begin again. You question your motives and your actions again and again. Meanwhile, the discharge planner is calling and calling.

Tick, tick, tick. You must start again. You call your second, third, and fourth choices. You are more educated, more knowledgeable. This time you ask about bed availability. You've figured out some of the logistics. This time you know more about finances. There seems to be a deposit, a nonrefundable entrance fee, all before the regular monthly fee. You've also learned to check how much notice is required before you can leave their institution. Is it thirty days? Sixty days? Six months? All of this matters. The details become overwhelming. How do you juggle all these facts? Do you just give up and choose the first facility that will take your loved one? Do you pick by location? Maybe there is a place close to the house, so you can charge over there to comfort your beloved when they don't successfully make the transition or adjust to the new situation.

A few reminders in this stage:

- When your beloved passes away, no one will throw you a victory parade, present you the key to the city, or pin a medal on your chest.
- Although it may be cliché to say it, taking care of someone with dementia is an all-day job. It really does take a village to maintain someone with dementia. No one can do this alone.

- Even though you may get some rest and respite while your loved one is in the facility, moving them to the facility is something you do *for* them, not *to* them. The facility has more and better resources for dealing with dementia, as well as for dealing with other health issues than you have at home.

- Your loved one will tell you they want to go home, that they will be fine at home. They will give you every reason they should go home. You must make this difficult decision.

We, the authors, found it helpful to remind ourselves that this is a business decision. Try to take the emotions out of the decision. Do the research, rate the facility, factor in how far it is from the house. Is it across the state line? Are the rules different?

For example, places like Kansas City and the Omaha metro area are in different states. Kansas administers Medicare and Medicaid differently than Missouri does. One family we know did the research and found that one side of the river had more liberal income limits and protected the primary home from Medicaid liens. As their dad was already showing indicators of dementia, they wanted to protect their mom's assets. They sold the big family house, moved Dad and Mom across the river into a newer, handicapped-accessible house. When Dad declined, Mom would be protected financially, and the newer house layout would mean she didn't have to move after Dad passed away.

You'll also want to determine if the staff has specialized training. Will they accommodate a special diet? Can they do sliding-scale insulin injections? Can they transport your loved one to the doctor or to physical therapy? If not, do they have in-house physical therapy? Will they accept your loved one as a patient? Is this facility the right fit for the stage and abilities of your beloved?

Money is always a factor. Ask if the facility will accept Medicaid payments in case you need the financial help later. Many facilities do not accept Medicaid payments, but fortunately, some do. If your finances are borderline, you may need to start in a Medicare facility and then transfer to a Medicaid facility.

The words "Medicare" and "Medicaid" are frequently used interchangeably. This is incorrect. Medicare is health insurance for senior citizens, and Medicaid is a public assistance program for low-income people. The rules and regulations are different for the two programs. Medicaid will pay for many things that Medicare will not. However, one must meet strict income and net worth criteria to be eligible for Medicaid.

Medicaid facilities are usually not as luxurious but should provide the same level of care. However, transitioning to Medicaid is confusing and complex. It also requires and has a five-year look back period to ensure the family has not recently transferred assets strictly to qualify for Medicaid. You may need a Medicaid consultant. Ask the discharge planner if there are consultants in the area. If not, go to the internet. Transitioning to Medicaid is a specialized process, and without help, the surviving spouse may be left destitute.

You will need to know how much this care will cost. There is generally a base cost for housing, food, janitorial costs, and so on. Then there will be a fee for a service package that will increase based on how much care your beloved requires. Big-city costs are generally higher than in smaller towns and rural areas, but they may have more facilities and more choices.

Larry and Laura lived in California with their daughter. Their son was in Texas.

When Laura was diagnosed with frontotemporal dementia, Larry did his research and found that long-term care in Texas was considerably less expensive than in California. Because of this, they moved to Texas. Larry bought a small townhouse and placed Laura in an Assisted Living facility near his new home. The family broke even the first month of Laura's care.

Tick, tick, tick. You still don't have a facility that will accept your beloved spouse or parent. The authors have found that we had to have four assessments from four facilities before we found one that would both accept our beloveds and that we thought would be a good fit.

What is the bottom line? Don't wait for a crisis. Start doing your research as soon as you get on the roller coaster. If you are getting close to the point of exhaustion, burnout, or utter frustration, it may be time to make the hard call and the difficult decision. When you begin to wonder if placement will be necessary, it is probably time. When space is available, get your loved one into the facility. If you wait until the last minute, there may not be a vacancy. Remember, you are your beloved's best asset, and it is in their best interest to preserve your health and sanity.

How do you get your beloved to agree to move into a facility? There is no right or wrong way to move someone. The fact that this person you love must now receive 24/7 care hurts. The fact that the patient sometimes does not go willingly adds insult to the hurt. It may require creativity on the part of the caregiver and the family. The professionals use terms like, "therapeutic fibs," or, "white lies." Many placements are started as a "temporary visit" or a respite for the family. It may be necessary to tell your beloved that they need to get their strength back, and they can get the therapy they need at a facility. Another story that has worked for some is to tell the beloved that the doctor is worried about their nutrition and weight loss (or gain) and wants to get some long-term data on their eating, nutrition, and exercise routines, and the only way this can happen is at a facility. It may be necessary to take the bullheaded approach and just keep talking to them until they agree to go, even if it is only long enough to get them to the facility.

Because Leah experienced hallucinations and delirium, she called the police to report abuse by her husband, Lonnie.

Because of this call, Lonnie was removed from the home. Leah was then alone and without care. Her best friend, Loretta, went to check on her. Loretta convinced Leah that she needed therapy to get stronger so she could manage the home on her own.

Leah agreed to visit the facility temporarily as an inpatient so she could get her strength back. Lonnie had previously made all the arrangements with the facility. Both Loretta and Lonnie knew Leah would never return home.

Lucy was unable to take care of herself. Her son's family had taken care of her for many years.

The situation was now to the point that the family was unable to meet all her needs. They took Lucy for a visit to the facility and introduced her to many of the residents. Earlier in the day, the family had moved some of her things into the room, so Lucy felt at home. While Lucy had a few the problems adjusting to the new facility and the strict schedule for breakfast, lunch, and dinner, with help from her family, she did adjust. Eventually, she did not remember her family home and began to regard the facility as her home.

When your family comes to the placement decision, you should not feel guilty. Facilities offer round-the-clock care and monitoring that you cannot provide. They also have multiple shifts so the staff can rest. If you continue to attempt to provide care on your own, you risk caregiver burnout.

CHAPTER 13

Married but Solo

As mentioned earlier, the twenty-first century has brought medical advances that have extended lifetimes ten, twenty, or even thirty years. And while the length and quality of one's life has improved, there are times when the person we married or our parents need special care because of myriad health issues, including dementia. Sadly, that can make you the one who no one notices because the rest of the world is focused on your husband/wife/partner/parent/significant other. The rest of the world is focused on how devastating dementia is to your family member. They don't notice how this disease affects you. They don't see your loss. Someone you loved and grew to depend on is now completely dependent on you. You are trapped in a cage with only one way out, the passing of your beloved.

Michelle spoke of her husband:

> I used to be scared Mitch would die. Now, after five years of caring for him, I am scared that he won't die soon, and he will continue to suffer.

You are in limbo. You are not single and free to socialize or travel. Nor are you divorced and free of the financial burdens of doctor's fees and special modifications to the house. This continues to be your responsibility. You are still married, but you are married to someone who is not here. There are no Christmas parties you can both attend, no traveling, no dances, or nights at the club. There is no companionship, no help with decisions, no one to talk to at night. And of course, there is no intimacy.

A measure of your success is having your health intact at the end of this journey. There will be no victory; nor is there any virtue in losing your life or your health. It will be difficult to carve out time and money for yourself. Try to do something that brings you pleasure or joy. Perhaps an online book club or Bible study. Maybe a monthly movie with the old gang or an hour at the gym. Whatever it is, do something for yourself. Even in a war, troops are routinely rotated out for rest and recuperation, R&R. You must allow yourself to have your own R&R. This is one way to maintain your strength and ability so you can advocate for your loved one. Just because your beloved has gone off the dementia cliff is no reason for you to be at the bottom, waiting for them to crush you when they hit bottom.

Doug Manning, in his book *When Love Gets Tough, the Nursing Home Decision,* suggests that the people who operate long-term care facilities have found that it is more difficult for husbands to place their wives in a facility than it is for wives to place their husbands. Whether this is due to the inherent physical differences between men and women or the perceived need for the husband to be the protector is not known. Regardless of the reason, it is another challenge to be faced, even if it is only in your mind.

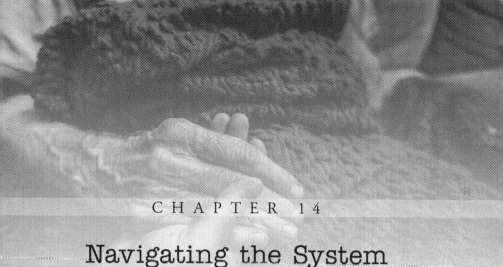

CHAPTER 14

Navigating the System

This chapter is not an exhaustive treatise on elder law. Neither of the authors is an attorney or involved in the legal profession. Nothing in this chapter should be considered legal advice. This chapter is a result of the authors' experiences dealing with dementia. Entire law school courses have been taught on this subject. This is only an overview of what you need and why you need it. As the caregiver, you must consider not only the person you care for but yourself as well. Everyone needs their documents in order. As stated elsewhere, you are your beloved's most valuable resource, and you must take care of yourself along with them.

Just because you are healthy now, there is no guarantee that you will outlive the person you are caring for; 63 percent of caregivers die before the people they care for (https://www.home2home4seniors.com › increased-mortality-rate-for-caregivers). Because others, especially your beloved and your family, are depending on you, your documents, especially your decisions, can be more important than you realize.

Wills, powers of attorney, advance medical directives, and end-of-life laws vary widely from state to state. This is not the time to go to the internet and download some generic forms. Stop reading this right now. Put this book down and make an appointment with an elder care lawyer before you are in crisis. If you are already in crisis, it is even more important to call your lawyer now. Make the time to develop the documents for yourself and your loved one. Yes, both you and the person you are caring for need these important documents.

Nadine divorced when her daughter, Natalie, was young. She supported herself and Natalie alone, with no child support.

> Nadine was immensely proud the day when she was able to buy a small house. She continued to work and support herself while Natalie went out into the world. All was going well. Then one day, Natalie came home in tears, pregnant! Nadine and Natalie decided the best thing would be to move into the house together, so Grandma Nadine could help raise the baby. When baby Nick was nine years old, the worst happened: Nadine had a mild stroke. Nadine and Natalie were both concerned that in the event of Natalie's death, Nick would end up in foster care and Nadine in a facility. A simple Will stating Nadine's wishes to give the house to Natalie and Natalie's Will giving custody of Nick to Nadine or a friend, relative, or neighbor would eliminate many of these concerns.

Part of caregiving is having one's own affairs in order. Every adult—anyone over the age of eighteen—should have a Will. This is worth repeating. *Every adult needs a will.*

Your Will

As stated previously, everyone needs a Will; no one will live forever. Your Will expresses what you want done with your estate after you are gone. If you die without a Will, called dying intestate, the disposition of your affairs and distribution of assets will be governed by the laws of your state. Your Will allows you to be specific about who or what charity or organization receives your money, your home, your business, and so on. For instance, you may want to donate part of your estate to an organization that has been a significant part of your life. Examples are organizations such as the Masons, the Scouts, a church, or a fraternal organization. Or you may have a child with special needs who requires more care than the others. You might give your half interest in your business to your partner, to your spouse, or to a dear friend. You might also list keepsakes to go to important people in your life. Your Will can direct these actions.

Nick and Nora met later in life. Because they were older and were not going to have children, they figured it would be easier just to live together rather than to get married.

Before Nick got dementia, he did not update his Will. After he was diagnosed, he was unable to understand the consequences of his Will or Power of Attorney documents, so they could not be changed. When he fell and needed hospitalization, Nora had to call Nick's brother, 1,500 miles away, and it was up to the brother to discuss his health care with the doctor. None of the doctors or nurses could discuss his condition with Nora because she was neither the spouse nor did she have Nick's Power of Attorney. When Nick died, the house that was titled in Nick's name only became the property of Nick's brother. He evicted Nora one Friday afternoon. She was left with none of the pleasant things the two of them had built together. Worse, she was homeless.

Your Will can be a relatively simple document, or it can be as complex as you wish. After you are gone, someone must do the paperwork and pay your bills. The executor is the person who makes sure your wishes are carried out. In many states, the term "executor" is being replaced with the term "personal representative." The executor and the attorney will file papers in the local probate court. The judge will approve the validity of your Will. The next step is for the attorney to give the court a list of your property, debts, and the people or organizations you listed to inherit your estate. Next, relatives and creditors are officially notified of your death.

If you are the executor or personal representative for your beloved, you must locate and manage the assets during the probate process. This usually takes a few months to a year. Depending on the assets in the Will and the amount of their debts, the executor may have to decide to sell real estate, securities, or other property. Without a proper Will, the owner has no say in what assets are sold or how the remainder of the estate is distributed.

You may be thinking, *What if I don't have a Will?* Without a Will, several things that you had control of go away. You put the courts in charge of the distribution of your estate. You do not get to choose who receives your assets. You do not get to choose who oversees your affairs. You do not get to choose who gets custody of your minor or special needs children. If your family lives a significant distance from you, it may place a burden on them and increase the cost of distributing your remaining assets.

Your next thought may be, *I don't have much anyway.* Even if this is the case, you may have keepsakes or family heirlooms you want to go to specific individuals. Maybe you own a firearm or jewelry collection that should not be broken up or should go to someone or an organization who is not a member of your family. Without a Will, these decisions are dictated by law, and any discretion is left to a judge who will be unfamiliar with you and your family, and whose flexibility is limited under the law. The old expression, "Your Will, Your Way," applies here.

Other necessary documents.

Three other important documents are a Power Of Attorney for your loved one's personal affairs, a Medical Power Of Attorney (MPOA), and a Do Not Resuscitate (DNR) order. These documents are different than a Will. A Will takes effect only after the person has died.

Power Of Attorney

A Power Of Attorney is for the in-between stage when an individual is sick or injured and not capable of making decisions for themselves. While the emphasis of this book is dementia, consider a car accident. A person may be incapacitated for several weeks and be unable to manage their personal affairs or participate in decisions regarding their treatment. Before an incident, while you are healthy and thinking well, you appoint your Attorney-In-Fact to act in your place when and if you are incapacitated. You can choose the person you feel is most capable to step in and take care of your personal affairs. You can name several people in case one is unable to take care of things. You may wish to name your spouse, then your best friend, and then your son or daughter. You can also name nonfamily members to deal with various aspects of your affairs.

Without a Power Of Attorney, in some states, no one except a spouse, or a court-appointed guardian can represent you or pay your bills. A judge will be required to appoint a conservator or guardian to manage your care and affairs. The court process requires your loved one to find and hire a lawyer and to ask the court's permission to appoint a guardian. This takes time and money that could otherwise be used to pay for nurses, medication, therapy, and so on. Without your wishes known before the need, the judge may not choose someone you know but instead assign an estate company to manage your affairs. This may result in additional costs to the family. All of this can be avoided by naming someone you trust in advance with a simple Power of Attorney.

A Power Of Attorney can be either "durable" or "springing." A durable Power Of Attorney takes effect immediately on being signed. That is, the moment it is signed, another person can do whatever the document allows them to do.

A springing Power Of Attorney takes effect only after a specified event occurs. The person who signs this document can specify what events or conditions must occur before the other person steps in. In many cases, the triggering event is a Declaration Of Incompetence. On the surface this may appear to be a preferred path, however as a practical matter, it is difficult to get someone declared incompetent; incapable of making their own decisions. An effective springing Power Of Attorney includes language that defines incapacitation and how to get someone, usually a family doctor or two treating doctors, to agree that the individual is incapacitated. A springing Power Of Attorney should state who will declare the individual incapacitated and whether it requires one or two doctors to declare incapacity. If this is not spelled out clearly, the decision could end up in court. Therefore, it is crucial to define what constitutes incapacitation for the purpose of the Power Of Attorney document.

The beauty of the durable Power Of Attorney is that it takes effect immediately and remains in effect if the signer becomes incompetent. The ugly part of a durable Power Of Attorney is the same; it takes effect immediately and remains in force. Unless the designated person is trustworthy, it is possible they would take action that is not in the best interest of the signer as soon as it is signed or anytime afterward. The designated person must be someone the signer trusts completely. This person must also be competent enough to understand the affairs and wishes of the signer.

A Power Of Attorney only allows the designated person to do what the signer specifies in the document. This can range from broad-ranging authority to buy and sell property, take on debt, etc., or it can be limited to something unique and specific, such as only the sale of one vehicle. More than one Power Of Attorney can be written. For example, one person, perhaps a business partner, can have authority to manage interest in a shared business, and another person, perhaps a spouse or child, can have authority over personal affairs.

Medical Power of Attorney (MPOA)

According to Legalboulevard.com, nearly 75 percent of Americans will someday be in a situation where they are unable to make medical decisions for themselves. The time to make these decisions is before the situation becomes urgent and doctors and nurses are asking for decisions. The MPOA is like the "normal" Power of Attorney except it pertains only to medical issues.

An MPOA can go by various names: health-care Power of Attorney, durable Power of Attorney for health care, health-care proxy, advanced-care directive, etc. Regardless of the name, the MPOA allows one person to make health-care decisions for another in the event the signer is incapacitated. Unlike the Power of Attorney for financial affairs, the MPOA only takes effect when the signer is unable to make their own decisions. Because the signer will be incapacitated when it takes effect, their wishes must be made clear in the document. This can be important if specific religious views or specific medical procedures should be included or prohibited. For example, a person may want to refuse a blood transfusion or specific surgical procedures or drugs. Other things that can be included are who is to make medical decisions in the event of incapacitation, where the individual is to receive health care, whether to continue nutrition or hydration, and when to stop any further intervention.

Living Will

While an MPOA grants the authority to speak on another's behalf, a Living Will outlines one's wishes for end-of-life care. The Living Will communicates and clarifies the individual's beliefs and values and makes it easier for the agent to make decisions based on previously stated preferences, relieving some of the stress the agent may experience.

Do Not Resuscitate (DNR)

A Do Not Resuscitate order (DNR), also known as "no code", is a special case of an MPOA. Its purpose is to let medical professionals know you do not want to be resuscitated if you go into cardiac arrest or stop breathing. People who are chronically ill often regard a DNR as a graceful way to leave the world on their own terms. The details of a DNR are usually discussed at the time of admission to a hospital, nursing facility, or hospice program.

While you and your beloved are both healthy and calm, take the time to have the difficult, complicated, and challenging talk about what you both want to have done. Once you and your loved one have decided, quickly make the appointment to talk to your lawyer. It may be easier to start the process by calling the lawyer first. Often people find the discussion too difficult to start without the lawyer starting it for them. The lawyer will then take you through many scenarios. The lawyer's job is to ask you about situations you may have never considered. The lawyer will develop the documents as you wish. Because these are difficult conversations, it may be tempting to be vague in the documents. This is not the time or place to be ambiguous. Assume that anything that can be misinterpreted will be.

Involving the entire family, even if it is over telephone or video conference, during this process will be time well spent. Make it clear to those family members who are not designated as agent that you expect them to allow the designated person to make decisions. This is not the time or place to attempt to resolve underlying family issues by requiring two people to agree on a course of medical treatment or how they should manage your financial affairs. Involving the family and those who will be named in the MPOA is critical.

In the authors' experience, when these issues are being discussed, too often people take the easy way out and say, "If there is no hope for me, pull the plug." That is the easy decision for both the patient and the loved one. The Living Will is meant to provide guidance to those patients who are in a gray area and for those who will be forced to make these complex decisions. For instance, should they authorize a feeding tube or a ventilator? Would you be comfortable with an experimental drug or a radical new surgery that may extend your life but would require you to be attached to a machine for an extended period? Do you wish to have CPR performed on you even if it will likely break your ribs, puncture a lung, and leave you with reduced physical function for the rest of your life? What heroic measures—such as ventilators, surgery, or other treatments—do you specifically authorize or not authorize?

Just because you have made all these decisions doesn't mean it will be easy on the loved ones, only that it will be easier.

Nadine and Nathan thought they had their medical decisions made.

Nadine and Nathan thought they had their medical decisions made. That was until Nathan had a stomach bleed. He had spent three days in intensive care, and his digestive system was shutting down. The doctors advised Nadine that the treatments were working, but they weren't working fast enough to save Nathan's life. To save him, she would need to authorize putting him on a ventilator. For the previous two years, he had made it clear to her that he did not want to ever be put on a ventilator. He believed that a ventilator only prolonged the inevitable. Nadine was faced with a difficult decision. Ultimately, she violated Nathan's wishes and authorized the ventilator for five days. At the end of five days, she withdrew the ventilator authority and allowed Nathan to die.

Nancy and Nick had been married for ten years when they began the process of preparing their MPOAs.

They knew that they would be spending time together as they aged. For this reason, they named each other as the first person in their MPOA. Then they both named others as the second and third people to make their decisions. Nancy named their niece and one of her former colleagues as second and third in line. When Nancy was placed in assisted living due to dementia, their lawyer advised Nick to resign as her agent so that he could go back to being the loving husband, and he could make the niece or Nancy's former colleague "the bad guy." The lawyer's thinking was that in her diminished capacity, Nancy would be more accepting of another's judgment than of Nick's. As soon as the niece was notified that Nick was resigning, the niece decided she did not want the responsibility of Nancy's care and promptly resigned. This made the former colleague responsible for Nancy's health care. When notified, the colleague was shocked and stated she had no knowledge of this and would not be responsible for managing Nancy's care or making decisions on her behalf. Nancy was left with no one to speak for her. Nick had to petition the court to appoint a guardian.

Once you have your documents in order, what do you do with them? The MPOA is not something that should be just signed and filed away. If your loved one is quite ill, has had a series of falls, or has a complicated medical history, you may need these documents quickly, so keep them nearby. The advice of many ambulance services is to keep the documents on the refrigerator. The refrigerator is where a first responder will go to look for these documents and a medication list. The authors have placed their documents in a plastic protective cover or envelope and used a magnet to keep them in place on their refrigerators.

Probate

Probate is the formal process that oversees the distribution of a deceased person's assets. The probate process involves several steps.

First, the judge will determine the validity of the Will. The question will be: Did your loved one legally create the Will and sign it appropriately? Second, the judge will approve the list of the assets and property of the deceased. Later the judge will ensure all bills, taxes, and other debts are paid. Considering all the legal publication requirements, court dates, lawyer fees, publication fees etc., probate generally takes a year or more. Yes, even death is expensive.

The judge will need to review all these documents, so your attorney will need to present these documents to the judge. You will have to pay your attorney. Then there will be court costs. To open probate is generally a few hundred dollars. After opening probate, the court costs range from $215 to over $1,200. In most states, the fee is determined by the value of the estate.

There are ways to avoid probate. Transfer on death accounts, beneficiary designations, and joint ownership are just a few of the ways assets can be passed to others without going through the probate process. As stated previously, each state is different, and each situation is different. An hour with an estate planning attorney will be money well spent. This is especially true if you or your spouse have been married more than once, have an unmarried domestic partner, have a special needs child, have family heirlooms, or any number of unique situations.

The hospital honored the DNR, and your loved one died. You thought you were prepared, but you find yourself in a stupor. You can hardly breathe with the loss. You've called the family, and you are hoping they will help you. Some families will help; some families won't. You made the funeral arrangements, and the pastor did a lovely service. But now what? How do you pay those hospital bills, and how do you go forward? Call the lawyer who prepared your documents for more complete directions. The estate planning attorney may direct you to a separate probate attorney. At this point, the investment you made earlier in the estate planning attorney can really pay off. The attorney managing your loved one's affairs will have a much easier time if all the documents are in order. For every reason in this chapter, an estate planning attorney can be worth much more than the fees they charge.

CHAPTER 15

Oh My God, What Are They Thinking?

Your beloved just accused you of stealing from them or having an affair in your home. Your loved one called the neighbor to complain about the radio playing the same song all night, and the neighbor is three states away. You and your loved one spent all day looking for their cell phone, hearing aids, or that special pen. Each search becomes an obsession. The world must stop until this problem is resolved.

All you want to do is get your loved one settled, so you can relax or catch up on some TV. You would love to have a conversation with the person they used to be. But they can't and won't leave you alone. They won't stop obsessing. What are they thinking?

The fact is the brilliant person you knew is *not* thinking. Their brain is deteriorating, and they cannot help themselves. And their capability is deteriorating more every day.

You will be asked the same thing, many times. You will try to answer it again with calmness and dignity. Getting short with them will only provoke them and thereby take longer to calm them down. Eventually, they may not even know who you are. You become, "that nice person who brings me treats." Worse, you may become a person who, in their mind, is out to do them harm. If you want to protect them, it may be necessary to love them from afar.

When Olivia was ready to leave the hospital, it was noted on her discharge records:

"Oscar, Olivia's husband, is a trigger for her paranoia anxiety. We do not recommend that they have contact at this time. We told the husband that he will have to "love her from afar," and he has accepted this.

Olivia was transferred from an Assisted Living facility to a Memory Care facility. Oscar would not see her for five months. Olivia became delusional and thought she had been kidnapped by benevolent captors who fed her and took care of her. Oscar was allowed to send her get well cards and treats. The staff assured her that he was fine and concerned about her. After five months, Olivia's dementia had progressed, and she had deteriorated further. The staff allowed Oscar to visit with supervision. Olivia was enthralled by his visit. She had progressed through the paranoia phase and no longer perceived Oscar as a threat. As a result, he was not the trigger of her fear any longer and was allowed to visit her for the remainder of her life.

The person with dementia may demonstrate personality changes. They may appear to have depression. They may become more apathetic about their appearance and completing daily tasks, or they may fail to see the consequences of their actions.

Owen and Opal were going to their granddaughter's wedding several states away.

Owen knew that it was too far to drive as Opal would once again be at risk of blood clots in her legs. Owen was also worried that the frequent stops at gas stations and for meals would allow Opal to wander off or get upset at the new and different surroundings. Owen made airline reservations to minimize the time that Opal would be immobile and possibly get blood clots. When Owen and Opal arrived at the airport, the airline provided an aide to push Opal through the airport. Connections were tight, and they would barely make it to the connecting flight if everything went well. Opal became so obsessed with getting to an ATM to get cash to tip the aide that they missed the connection. They wound up waiting in the airport for three hours for the next flight because of her obsession.

Dementia patients have limited capacity to think. The paranoia and obsessions are all manifestations of the dementia. The brain breaks down, and the patient gets stuck thinking the same thing over and over. No amount of rational discussion will help. Rather than try to cajole or convince them to do something, change the subject slightly. The best way to cope may be to try to distract and redirect. A little fiblet, such as, "There will be an ATM machine down the hall," or, "I already tipped the aide," will make your life easier. Little white lies are the caregiver's friends and not to be worried about.

CHAPTER 16

Planning and Preparing

You have been given a huge challenge. You have no idea what you are facing. You are already behind. You need to get your collective paperwork together, and you need to do it now. The quicker you realize you are dealing with the challenge of your life, the more effective an advocate you will be. You and your beloved have much to do, and you need to start now.

No one knows how long your beloved has left to live. More important, no one knows how long they will be competent to execute (sign) legal documents. If you wait too long, your attorney may decide your beloved is not competent to make legal decisions. If this happens, it may be necessary for a judge to assign a guardian. If you have been discussing your or their estate plan, a diagnosis of dementia should be the nudge to get you to your attorney's office. Do not wait until you think the end is near or they have deteriorated further. Ancient wisdom tells us that the best time to plant a tree is yesterday. The next best time to plant a tree is today. Today is the best time to complete your legal documents.

There is also a difference between having the ability to sign one's name and the mental capacity to understand what is being signed. If your beloved does not have the physical ability to sign their name, they can direct someone else to sign on their behalf. They can also make a mark, provided it is properly witnessed. However, the most important thing to remember is the mental capacity to understand the document, in other words, its effect. These are legal tests that your attorney should know.

Many years ago, a Will could simply state, "I, John Doe, being of sound mind…," and that was sufficient to meet the legal standard. However, in recent years, it has been determined that this language is insufficient. One must meet an objective legal standard of being able to understand what they are signing. The mental capacity of a person with dementia can fluctuate. However, "better than yesterday," is not sufficient. The person must meet the legal standard in your state.

You should begin preparing for long-term care placement by contacting and visiting elder care facilities and interviewing their staff. You need to know their costs and their services. If you can meet or call other families who have a loved one in the facility, your fears will hopefully be reduced.

You should begin learning everything you can about dementia and caregiving. Reading this book is a good first step. The resources at the end are other places to help your education. Dementia has no timeline; no one can look at a medical chart and tell you when the next phase of your beloved's journey will start. When the doctor diagnoses dementia, you will not receive a sticker with an expiration date. You will have to consider and prepare for every eventuality.

It is not pleasant to bring up things like long-term care, estate taxes, probate, hospice, and Wills when you have just learned that someone you love is deteriorating. Welcome to reality. In modern parlance, this is called "adulting."

Although discussions about funerals and memorial services are not critical to your day-to-day activities, these discussions may help you in the future. But if you can get your beloved to begin discussing and then decide what kind of funeral service would be meaningful to them, it might head off future family battles. No one can see the future. No one knows how long anyone has. Start now!

If you did not do it in the previous chapter, put this book down and get both your beloved's and your own affairs in order now.

CHAPTER 17

Questioning

Taking care of someone you love who has dementia will be one of the most challenging things you will do. You will make thousands of decisions, each one more difficult than the last. If you are taking care of a spouse who has children from a previous relationship, they will question your decisions. If you are caring for your parents, your siblings will question you. You will question yourself. Friends will offer advice. All of this will cause you to question yourself again and again.

You will wonder if you are doing the right thing. Friends, neighbors, and family will ask questions, and you will often feel as if they are interrogating you. You will begin to feel as if they don't trust you. Of course, none of them is willing to come help for a day either. They are just making conversation. Or maybe they truly don't understand what is happening with your beloved. But it doesn't feel that way. When they begin to ask pointed questions, simply suggest they take a week off work to help with feeding, transferring, toileting, and attending doctor's appointments. Then you can politely suggest they research this diagnosis before they ask.

As long as you are taking care of them with a loving heart and a kind spirit, you are doing the right thing. No one else knows everything you do about your beloved's condition, what sets them off, or what calms them down. Some relatives will refuse to believe you are caring for a person with a terminal disease. After all, they look fine, they are not in a hospital, and they don't have tubes and lines coming out of them. So, they must be fine. You know better!

If your beloved appointed you as their Power Of Attorney, they had special trust and confidence in you and your levelheadedness. Use it. Don't believe the family's, neighbors', or nosy church people's comments. Don't live in last week or last month. Let them question. Answer politely with only the minimum amount of detail necessary. Make your decisions and move forward. The only explanation you need to give these outsiders is, "This is what the doctor and I think is best." If they persist in questioning your decisions, suggest they contact the Alzheimer's Association or join an online dementia chat group. (See chapter 6, "Family, Friends, and Flying Blind.")

Your parents are special. You won't get a replacement mom or dad. As you care for them, you will continue to question yourself. Your extended family will question your actions, especially when you can't care for them anymore or know they aren't safe at home. Your sisters, brothers, aunts, and uncles will be sure you are being selfish. But your parents' safety is the most important thing to think about. You will cry bucketloads of tears before this is over. As Dorothy from the *Wizard of Oz* said, "There's no place like home." Your parents may have lived in that house for years, and you may have grown up there. But Mom is having trouble with the stairs, and Dad needs more help too. They could probably use some more company. Dad's dementia has gotten worse, so there is no one for mom to talk to, no conversations of substance. But after soul-searching and questioning yourself, you will wonder if you did enough. You will ask yourself, *"Could I have done more? What should I have done differently? How do I keep going?"* As they decline, you will have to keep going. You will be tired and lonely. Remember to care for yourself. Don't question yourself. Know that you are doing your best. As long as you take care of them with love in your heart, you are doing the right thing.

CHAPTER 18

Responses: Yours and Theirs

When your beloved enters the belligerent stage, usually in the middle stage of dementia, they will lash out at you for the smallest things. Some things will be real; others will be imagined. Your loved one may have intense feelings of anger that may move to violent aggression. Violent behaviors may begin with early warning signs, such as raising their voice or using foul language you have never heard them use before. Other middle-stage behaviors may include repetitive motions, such as stacking and restacking silverware, cards, poker chips, or other items. Sometimes a fidget board or other distractive device can keep them occupied.

Obsessive-compulsive behaviors such as hoarding may drive you, the caregiver, crazy. At this stage, they still notice if you throw their things away. If you do have to make the path through the living room wider, (and therefore safer), their anger and aggression are likely to escalate. They may even mimic hitting you by swinging their fists. Certainly, they are angry and may yell at you and throw things in your direction.

The anger will sometimes seem to come out of the blue. This unprovoked anger can be the most difficult to cope with. It is normal to feel hurt and discouraged. This will enflame your own anger. As your beloved's caregiver, it can be helpful to remind yourself that you love them and that the disease—not the individual—is responsible for this behavior. The brain also controls our emotions and behaviors. Depending on the type of dementia, their emotions may be affected as well.

Others will tell you, "It is not them; it is the disease." You will hear this so often you will get sick of hearing it. They will still look like the person you used to know and love. It may help to remind yourself that the person you knew has been replaced by this brain-damaged, demented lunatic.

Different types of dementia damage different areas of the brain. Someone with a brain injury from an accident or a stroke can have damage in more than one area of the brain. Lewy body dementia increases the likelihood of delusions and hallucinations. Loved ones with frontotemporal dementia may exhibit physically aggressive behavior far earlier than other patients with dementia diagnoses. This is because the damaged frontal lobe of the brain is where emotional control is located. Empathy, impulse control, and judgment can be lost. This leads to impulsiveness and violent behaviors. Unfortunately, delusions tend to occur in later stages of dementia for everyone. Alzheimer's patients retain self-control longer than patients with other types of brain damage, but they lose their short-term memories earlier.

Paranoia, delusions, and hallucinations can be difficult symptoms for the caregiver to manage. Consider how dieting can affect a fully functioning person's mood, energy level, and thinking. In people with dementia, everyday hunger can lead to sudden outbursts or aggressive impulses. When you think an outburst is coming soon, you may want to offer a meal or snack your beloved enjoys.

When trying to manage their anger and aggression, remember that pain, fatigue, hunger, or overstimulation can be factors. Think about their day. It is probable that driving to two doctor's appointments and then a visit to the lab for a blood draw could be too much for your loved one. If this is the case, life might be easier if you lower the stimulation level by spreading out stimulating activities over several days, offer them an over-the-counter pain reliever, and/ or bring them a snack.

Another potential cause for an angry outbreak is a Urinary Tract Infection or UTI. Because the dementia reduces their mental capacity, many patients cannot verbalize that something is wrong, so they react by lashing out at anyone. This can be exacerbated by delirium. It is almost routine for caregivers to suspect a UTI when behavior changes for the worse. Interestingly, UTIs among the elderly are sometimes misdiagnosed as dementia. Dementia patients are at increased risk for UTIs because of their reduced ability to take care of their own personal hygiene, compounded by reduced control of their bladder and bowels.

> Ruth had been married to Robert for forty-six years. She was a war bride and suffered greatly in Germany during the World War II. She followed Robert to the United States, where they built a life together.

>> When she began to talk about the soldiers outside the house, Robert tried to reassure her. But no matter how much he comforted her, the anxiety and fear were uncontrollable. Eventually, Ruth was unable to recognize him. Ruth saw Robert as a soldier who wanted to hurt her. She acted first, stabbing Robert in the chest with a kitchen knife. Despite his severe injury, Robert was still able to call 911. Robert recovered but was no longer able to care for his beloved wife. He declined to press charges for attempted murder, but Ruth was involuntarily and permanently moved to a Memory Care unit.

Because of diminished capacity, routines and daily habits may make your life easier. If your loved one gets up at the same time every day, eats breakfast, and then showers and dresses in the same order, it may be easier for them to keep this routine when they are belligerent or continue to decline. Many patients struggle in the evening hours. (See Chapter 10, Jargon and Terms, and Chapter 19, Showtiming and

Sundowning.) If your beloved is more angry and more frustrated in the evening, consider moving activities like showering to the morning.

When someone with dementia lashes out at you for seemingly no reason, it's normal to feel embarrassed, shocked, hurt, or angry. Trying to figure out the causes of the anger may help you to defuse the situation before it starts or how to best to respond. While this may work, it may also be a complete waste of time as the anger might be triggered by something in the past or a hallucination. Misunderstandings are common because dementia affects the communication area of the brain. Unless you have the patience of Job, you will get angry! You are working hard, getting no recognition for your efforts, and you are tired.

Your loved one may have trouble understanding what is going on or staying on track with a conversation. This can be especially true at the doctor's office. As a caregiver, you may think it is helpful to have these important discussions with your beloved present, but you may notice agitation, repetitive behaviors, and anger building. Your beloved might not understand the conversation and feel that you and the doctor are trying to boss them around. If this is the case, take time later in the day, or the next day, to review the doctor's orders and explain why the doctor wants to change the medications, for example.

The internet has several tests and suggestions concerning anger. The Multidimensional Anger Test comes from IDR Labs. It consists of thirty-eight questions that ask you to reflect on your experiences with anger. It's meant to evaluate your susceptibility to feelings of anger (https://www.verywellhealth.com/anger-and-aggression-in-dementia-4134488).

These types of tests are not perfect but may help you to understand your own mental state so that you can cope with your beloved in a kind and compassionate way. Your anger is an early warning sign that you need to rethink how to solve your current problem. Possibly you need to set firm boundaries with friends or family. It may be necessary to communicate more carefully with your loved one or bring in respite care for your own piece of mind.

Caregivers must guard against anger—righteous or not—so the anger does not explode in an aggressive, ugly way. When you are tired, have answered the same question a hundred times a day, and dealt with your belligerent loved one, you may drift into aggression. It is not easy to talk about how frustrated and how angry you feel. It helps if you have a friend in the same caregiving situation. Both the caregivers and the patient may benefit from time away to vent some of these feelings. However, it's not always easy to get away or find a sympathetic ear and talk about angry feelings. Therapists can be found at a reasonable cost at your local mental health center. A trained individual may help you to process your anger, think about it in new ways, and find some solutions that may work for your family. Additionally, online message boards can be convenient places to vent one's anger and gather techniques to defuse potentially hostile situations.

Helpful Suggestions

Here are other responses that you, as the caregiver, may find helpful. Depending on the situation, try one of these strategies when faced with anger or aggression.

- Remember that the person living with dementia may have a hostile outlook on life. If your personal space is invaded on the street at night, you become uncomfortable. Similarly, if the patient doesn't understand why, you are getting so close to them, you can expect resistance or combativeness. When care is necessary, try retreating a little and telling your beloved what care you need to provide, such as a shower or bringing them a glass of water so they can take their medications.
- More than one person approaching someone with dementia can raise anxieties and trigger aggression. Rather than having two or three people help you to get your beloved into the shower, use one person if possible.
- You might be so angry that you try to explain your side of the situation. Proving your point with someone who has dementia is rarely effective. In fact, you will probably just make your loved one even angrier. They will perceive that you are

arguing with them. As Dale Carnegie said, "You cannot win an argument." Instead, join their world. If they say something is bothering them, ask them about it, distract them, or redirect their thinking. A simple, "Let's talk about this tonight, when we have more time," may be enough to move them off the issue.

- For similar reasons, don't get bossy with them. You may know you are the rational, thinking one, and you just need them to do what you say. However, your loved one's mental state is deteriorating to that of a child in an adult's body. They need to be led and encouraged, not directed.

- If you are trying to get someone to brush their teeth and they become angry with you, leave them alone and give them a little time. They will often come to you in a few minutes and want help. Allowing a little time to pass can sometimes produce a completely different result.

- During a tantrum, you may be at your wit's end. Music can be a wonderful distraction. Try playing their favorite big band collection or soothing music. Sit with them for a few minutes before completing care. This may help get them dressed and get to that appointment on time. If nothing else, it may get them to calm down or even calm their anger. Dementia patients can turn on and off like a switch. Many dementia patients continue to respond to the rhythm of music until late in the disease.

When people are angry, they are in part irrational. When angry, people often talk rapidly. Rather than listen to any arguments, they are busy thinking up their responses. When you are aware of this in your own body and mind, force yourself to slow down and recognize your beloved is not fully there. Accepting that your loved one's condition is the cause may help you to feel calmer. Talking to someone about your daily life can be healing. In some cases, it will help you feel closer to your beloved.

CHAPTER 19

Showtiming and Sundowning

You have spent weeks taking care of them. You have answered the same question a hundred times: "What day is it?" "Where are my glasses?" "When is Jack coming to visit?" (Jack died ten years ago.) They have complained about the way you put them to bed last night, the way you made breakfast this morning, the weather outside, and the way President So and So is running the country (President So and So has been out of office for at least eight years.) Your nerves are worn to their ends.

Today is the big day! A doctor's appointment! Your heart is filled with hope. Finally, you will get some answers to what demon has possessed this person you love and how to remove it. You spend more than an hour getting your loved one showered, dressed, and into the car. When you get to the doctor's office, they come on like a light. They are charming, rational, even lucid. In the exam room, they are completely there. They call the doctor by name, they know what day it is, they can tell the route they took to get to the office. They even know what they had for dinner last night. You are confused! You wonder what just happened. Where did this person come from? After the exam, you get a snack. Again, they are charming. It is as if the disease never existed. Yet by the time you get home, they are exhausted, so they take a nap. Tomorrow it all starts again.

This is called showtiming. The best analogy is that the mind is like a muscle. Normally muscles have a certain ability but, when necessary, can be pushed to do more. The muscle will be overworked and ache the next day. In the doctor's office, at the restaurant, or when visitors come over, the mind can be pushed beyond its normal limits. The patient can be charming and witty. Then when the need to perform is over, they crash, and they crash hard, sometimes sleeping for eighteen or more hours. When they wake up, they have declined even more.

This is confusing to the caregiver. You wonder, *Why can't they be like that with me?* This is just another part of the disease you must deal with. Much like a runner who is giving it his all, our loved ones can dig deep within themselves for that little extra when it is necessary. But they cannot do it for long. They have reduced brain capacity.

What can you do about showtiming? The short answer is not much. You just need to be ready for it. Knowing that it is going to happen will reduce your frustration. The other thing that sometimes helps is to sit behind them when they visit the doctor. When they tell the doctor they are fine, you can shake your head no. You can also send the doctor other signals from behind them. Like hurricane season in the tropics or winter in the north, showtiming is something you can't do much about. Just know it is coming, be aware, and be ready for it.

Sundowning is related to showtiming, but it goes the other way. Instead of your beloved being aware and engaged, they become confused and agitated. Sundowning is sometimes called late-day confusion. It is not an illness but a set of behaviors that tend to occur later in the day. Whether sundowning is related to lack of light or mental exhaustion after a stressful day is not clearly known. Many suspect that it is a combination of physical fatigue, poor sleep quality, hunger, thirst, physical discomfort (too hot, too cold, incontinence, etc.), and the cognitive demands of living and switching from one task to another. It is easy for a family member to remember them as they were—the aware and engaged adult—and want to bring that person back. The reality is that their mind cannot make that leap. Any attempt to exceed their newly reduced mental capacity will be met with confusion and agitation.

At the end of the day, a home caregiver can become fatigued, irritated, and burned out. The same can be said for a caregiver in a facility at the end of a shift. Because the caregiver is tired, they can unintentionally get short or abrupt with the patient. This can then be met with agitation or confusion on the part of the patient. These behaviors can then snowball on both the caregiver and the patient.

CHAPTER 20

Trust Your Support System

When you were born, you trusted your parents. These early years allowed you to grow up strong and dependable. When you were an adult, you began to date. Then you met "the one." You dated, married, and moved in together. Your trust grew. You and your spouse trusted each other, and that trust grew deeper over time. True intimacy requires trust. Trust grows and develops into a pool that extends and supports other emotions such as compassion, empathy, and love. They are all supported by that pool of trust.

Then that insidious thing called dementia moved into your lives. Your beloved got belligerent, and your feelings were hurt. Every temper tantrum, every insult, every time you were ignored or when they questioned your judgment yet again, the pool of trust continued to drain. You are moving out of the trust phase and into the belligerent phase. You must increasingly depend on your own judgment. It is hard to know if your beloved is experiencing delusions or hallucinations.

Tina and Thomas had been happily married for thirty-eight years. They were always close, doing everything together. They even worked together at their plumbing business. Tina answered the phone, did the books, and helped with the walk-in customers. Thomas scheduled the crews, ensured the inventory was reordered, and managed estimates.

But now Tina was sure her husband was having an affair:

She was heartbroken. Her beloved husband was cheating on her. Tina told everyone around her that Thomas had a girlfriend. All her friends were shocked. Tina and Thomas were the "perfect couple." They adored each other. They both helped with Thomas's elderly, widowed mother. They did everything together. How could Thomas be stepping out on Tina after all these years?

Thomas always tried to be the "perfect husband." He was kind and supportive even before Tina was diagnosed with dementia. Thomas was not yet able to retire and could not quit as they needed some money coming into the house. After working all day, Thomas came home, microwaved two dinners, and cleaned up the kitchen mess that Tina created during the day. Next, he got Tina into the shower. After getting her ready for bed, they would try to spend time together watching TV. When Tina would start nodding off, Thomas would tuck her in and kiss her goodnight. Finally, Thomas would have a few minutes to himself.

Poor Thomas. He had absolutely no energy left. Yet he had to take care of his elderly mother. Thomas tried to take his mom to lunch every Thursday and to church on Sunday. Church was getting to be a burden. Mom was moving slower and slower. Between trying to get Mom safely up the church stairs and trying to watch Tina so she didn't wander off, Sunday services did not restore his soul.

Thomas knew he was exhausted, too exhausted to do anything else. He wondered how Tina thought he ever had the time or energy to have an affair. Yet Tina was convinced that there was another woman. She would endlessly yell and insult Thomas about his fling every night, all night.

By this time, Thomas's pool of trust was drained. Fortunately, Thomas's emotions were replaced by his sense of duty, responsibility, obligation, and commitment. Thomas kept working, kept microwaving those meals, kept helping Tina shower and dress. Thomas kept showing his ongoing love when everything else was gone.

Thomas's trust in Tina was gone, and he no longer wanted to trust Tina's demented view of the world. Nor should he. Thomas had to trust and depend on the judgment of the professionals, his doctors, the social workers, the attorneys, their in-laws, and so on. Thomas had to put his trust in others.

So many times, we are unaware of where help might come from. It may be the pharmacist who notices your beloved is taking two similar medications. The double dose may aggravate many of the symptoms that are causing so many difficulties. It may be your auto mechanic, who notices a loose bolt. Neither of you know that as he tightens up everything, he prevented an accident that would have injured you and left your beloved without care.

Or maybe it is the retired military neighbor who tells you about the services offered at the Veterans Administration. Or maybe you never know who helped you. That person did the best possible thing at a moment in the past. They may tell you they were just doing their job, but they did it with care, diligence, and maybe even perfection.

Charles Plumb was a US Navy jet pilot in Vietnam. After 75 combat missions, his plane was destroyed by a surface-to-air missile. Plumb ejected and parachuted into enemy hands. He was captured and spent 6 years in a communist Vietnamese prison.

Years later, when Plumb and his wife were sitting in a restaurant, a man at another table came up and said, "You're Plumb! You flew jet fighters in Vietnam from the aircraft carrier Kitty Hawk. You were shot down!"

"How in the world did you know that?" asked Plumb.

"I packed your parachute," the man replied.

"Later Plumb pointed out that he needed many kinds of parachutes when his plane was shot down over enemy territory. He needed his physical parachute, his mental parachute, his emotional parachute, and his spiritual parachute."

(https://www.indres.com/news/who-packs-your-parachute-a-true-story-about-charles-plumb)

We all need help. Sometimes we need a parachute to float us down to a gentle landing. Sometimes it is from a church member who helped get Mom up the stairs and to her seat. Maybe it is someone who says, "Hello," "Please," and, "Thank you," making your day a little easier. Maybe it is the coworker who congratulates you on something you completed at work. Maybe it is the compliment on how nice you look today. Sometimes it is a server or cab driver who understands and says just the right thing that gives us the strength to persevere one more day. Remember that you are part of a larger system, the proverbial village, that will hopefully float us to a soft landing on our darkest days.

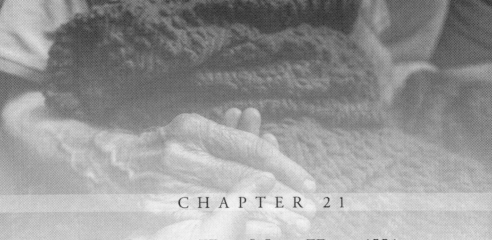

CHAPTER 21

Undone, Unable, Unwilling, Unfocused, Unappreciated

Every full-time caregiver feels tired and unappreciated. When you as a caregiver start to feel unwilling to heat that cup of coffee one more time or wash one more load of laundry, you may be in the "U" stage. Yes, there is another stage, the "undone" stage. You may feel that pieces of yourself have drifted away. Your energy is gone. All you can talk about is the disease, the doctor's appointments, and the medications. All your internet searches are for things like dementia, Frontotemporal, Lewy body, Alzheimer's, Medicare, Medicaid, and physical therapy. No wonder all your friends have drifted away.

You may not be clinically depressed, but you are struggling. You struggle to get the most minor tasks started. Once that load of laundry is started, it may stay in the washer another day or two or three. Then it becomes smelly and must be rewashed. Something else remains undone. Some would call it exhaustion; others call it burnout. But it's more than any of these. It is not fixable with pills, although antidepressants may help. It is the lack of focus that makes solving a minor problem feel impossible. You may lack focus to see a task to completion. You bought a lovely roast for Sunday dinner. You always set the table before you start dinner. But you can't because the dishes in the dishwasher are dirty. You are unable to get yourself to run the dishwasher. You just don't have the emotional or physical energy to do one more task. Dinner isn't started, and your loved one is hungry, so it's microwave meals yet again. Your loved one isn't pleased about the casual Sunday meal, and you feel discouraged and unloved. Once again you are unable, unappreciated, undone.

More importantly, your sense of self has gone. You feel undone, without hope, without a future. You remember your plans for the trip of a lifetime to Paris, a place you always wanted to visit. You are then jerked back to reality. You know you won't go without your beloved. Your long-held wishes and desires have evaporated. You are not the same person you once were. You don't have the same hopes or dreams. In fact, you don't have any hopes or dreams. You are stuck in the grind of cooking, cleaning, caring, and calming.

You miss the person you knew, but that person is not here and is not coming back. What will you feel like when they are completely gone? When they have gone to heaven or gone to a nursing home? Most days you are sad. The feelings you have are those of anticipatory grief. You are not grieving because they have died. No, you are grieving the loss of the competent loving partner, friend, or parent.

Undone will pass. There is life after dementia. But it is a different life. You may decide to sell the house and move. You may want to move to someplace without all those memories. You may decide to go back to work in a different city or move closer to the grandkids. Maybe you will choose to go to work at McDonalds just to get yourself out of the house. You will be forever changed by dementia, but there is life afterwards. Keep grinding though the chores of taking care of your loved one and try to think of something pleasant every day. These little memories of your loved one's smile or how much your beloved enjoyed watching the snow fall or the birds that came to the feeder. These memories will be with you always. These memories will be your treasures.

CHAPTER 22

Victories

This is a short chapter as victories are few. But we must celebrate whenever possible. Do your best to celebrate any little victory. Sometimes a victory is getting your loved one dressed in the morning without a battle. Sometimes it's getting their pajamas on and getting them to bed, so you can have a few minutes of quiet to yourself. Sometimes it's getting to watch an entire TV program without someone calling you. Sometimes it's getting your loved one to the toilet without mess. Yah! No Blue Glove Club today!

The most precious victories are the cognitive moments when you can reminisce about beautiful times in the past. The cute thing your child did. The trip to the lake with your friends. That time when you both did the perfect thing for a troubled friend. That wonderful person you love is still in there. These moments give you hope and energy to keep going, to keep loving them, keep caring for them. You do love them even in their worst, most belligerent moments.

The movie *The Notebook* was an excellent portrayal of dementia. An elderly man, played by James Garner, reads a couple's life story from a journal written by his elderly wife, played by Gena Rowlands, in the early stages of dementia. The man reads the same stories to her every day without fail. He reads the journal to help her remember their life together, but she doesn't remember. One day as he is reading, she recognizes him. They dance to "their song." But she doesn't remember for long, not even to the end of the dance. These are the precious victories. These are the moments you will treasure. Try to remind your loved one of the precious memories, those that define your relationship. These moments define you both as a couple, as parents, as good friends to each other.

What do you do now? Take lots of pictures. Take pictures of them asleep in the recliner. Take fun pictures of grandkids on their lap, of opening presents on Christmas Day, of birthdays, of Mother's and Father's Day. Take fun pictures.

Use your smartphone to record them telling the stories of their life. You may have to prompt them, but it's worth it. Where were they born? Who were their parents? Ask them about their brothers and sisters. Walk them through their life. Ask about grade school, high school, military service, jobs, and careers. Recording these stories will take time. You can do a little bit every day or every other day. Later you can replay the video when one of you needs cheering up. Or you can share it with the family.

But you know at some point you will be alone. Either your loved one will be in a care facility or gone to heaven. Take some of the not-so-fun pictures. Take pictures of them being angry, with their face contorted and their fist raised to hit you. Pictures of them in a bib with food down the front. Take some pictures of them with a slack jaw in the worst throws of dementia. You don't need to share these ugly pictures. But you will need them later. Later, when you are overcome with guilt, when you don't think you did enough, when you review and relive the past, you will need a reality check. The ugly pictures will remind you, … *you did do enough!* You did all you could do at that moment in time. You did everything you could for the person you loved. You loved them fully.

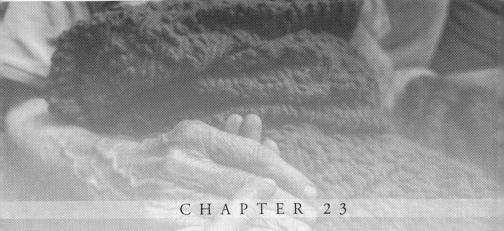

CHAPTER 23

Wheelchairs, Walkers, and Whatchamacallits

In the beginning, trivial things will help you manage. Rather than wonder if they took all the pills and all the right pills this morning, you will be able to tell at a glance with a medication box. Most people start their medications one at a time. The doctor starts them on something, and they get used to taking that one pill straight out of the prescription bottle. Then another medication bottle, and that too works into the everyday habits of life. Eventually there are seven or eight bottles. Then you run out of one of them. This is a minor crisis, yet a crisis that must be addressed. You must call the pharmacy and explain, begging for an immediate refill. Of course, the pharmacy has heard this before. But as you are a regular client, they expedite your refill. When this happens twice, it's time to move to the pill box.

Pill Boxes

Pill boxes come in one, two, three, and four-times-a-day boxes. If your loved one takes medications four times a day, get the big one. Also consider getting enough boxes for two or three weeks. That way when you are laying out the medications, you will note that the supply of the what's-its-name pills is low, and you can reorder. The pharmacy will appreciate your diligence, and you will be able to see your loved one took the right medications at the right time. This is one way to reduce your stress level.

As your loved one's dementia progresses, the number of medications will increase. An automatic pill dispenser may be necessary. These dispensers are frequently round with internal wedges to hold the pills. The pharmacist or nurse may have to help you program and lock the dispenser the first time. The dispenser can be set to beep prior to dispensing medications once, twice, three, or four times a day, or whenever medication is required. Most machines beep loudly and perpetually until the medication is dispensed. As a safety precaution, the dispenser can be locked and only dispense the medication as programmed, helping to prevent an inadvertent overdose. Depending on how many medications your loved one takes, most machines can hold a week of medications. Many come with extra storage, so a second week can be set up with minimal effort. As before, the pharmacy will appreciate the timely order, and you will know that your beloved is getting the proper medication at the proper time.

Shower Stools

Another helpful device is a shower stool. These come in many sizes and shapes. Most are plastic with an antimicrobial surface. They all come with nonslip caps on the feet. You will need to measure to be sure they will fit in your shower or bathtub. As your loved one's dementia progresses, you may need to move to a chair with arms. The arms allow your beloved to push themselves into a standing position. Additionally, there are benches that go over the outside of a bathtub. These allow your loved one to sit down and lift one leg at a time into and out of the tub. These benches are less portable and harder to move, but they may be perfect for keeping your beloved at home longer.

Bars and Handrails

Bars and handrails can be placed inside the bathtub or shower, on stairs, or near doors or steps. They are helpful to steady oneself while digging keys out of pockets or purses and unlocking doors. They are more useful than most people expect. When properly installed, they can enhance the appearance of a home.

Toilet Modifications

Toileting is one of the five Activities of Daily Living (ADLs). If your loved one can continue to get to the toilet by themselves, and use the facilities uneventfully, their dignity will remain intact. Plus, you won't have to clean anything! Bars around the toilet will assist them with getting onto and off the toilet. When getting up becomes a struggle, it will be time to install a raised toilet seat. This is an inexpensive plastic device about five inches tall. It is shaped like a toilet seat and sits on the ceramic bowl. Later, a raised toilet seat with bars (more like a chair) will become useful.

As time passes, it may be beneficial to install a taller toilet, or a toilet riser designed to fit between the toilet and the floor. These are sturdy and appear more normal than a toilet riser. Taller toilets are more expensive and will probably require professional installation. The other devices go over the existing toilet bowl.

Bidets

When incontinence, especially incontinence of bowel, becomes a regular occurrence, you will find yourself joining what is euphemistically called "the Blue Glove Club." You may spend much of your time cleaning up your beloved. It may be time to install either a bidet or a bidet attachment. Cleaning up after an incontinence incident is neither quick nor easy. A bidet can help rinse the skin in hard-to-reach areas. If you choose a bidet attachment, it will be less expensive than a stand-alone bidet, but the water temperature will be tepid. Bidet attachments are regularly available at hardware stores and home centers. Installing one is generally within the skills of a competent do-it-yourselfer. However, as a caregiver, you may want to contact a plumber or handyman to install it to avoid distractions while caring for your beloved.

Electric bidets require an electric outlet and a hot water line for the unit. They generally have temperature and pressure adjustments for maximum comfort. Installing an electric bidet should only be attempted by a professional.

Canes and Walkers

Canes and walkers will soon be coming into your home. Dementia, strokes, and old age diminish one's ability to maintain balance. Although your loved one may fight getting the cane, you should celebrate. A cane will extend their ability to be independent. It won't help them button their shirt, but it will help them get to the closet. It won't help them inside the shower, but it will help them get to the bathroom timely, saving you from the Blue Glove Club.

When balance issues progress, physical therapists may suggest a four-wheel walker. Your beloved will probably fight the walker even more than the cane. One suggestion is to stress that the four-wheel walkers have a seat. When you go out, they can stop and rest in the walker's seat. The walker will be convenient for them, and it will be easy for you to give it a quick wipe to sanitize it.

Eventually, canes and four-wheel walkers will no longer be enough. A four-wheel walker will roll out from someone who cannot stand up straight and maintain their balance on their feet. Physical therapists will likely want to transition your loved one to a two-wheel walker. A two-wheel walker has wheels in the front and pedestal legs in the back. This is more stable. When the patient starts to fall forward, their weight is transferred to the more stable legs. Without front wheels, it is less likely that the walker can slip away from them. The two-wheel walker should—might, hopefully—keep them from falling.

Most caregivers will deal with falls. These are frightening for both the caregiver and the person who falls. The first question to ask is, "Is this just a fall or did they break a hip?" If your beloved doesn't complain about moderate to severe pain, you can help them up. However, any fall with severe pain, disorientation, or a head injury requires a call to 911.

Wheelchairs

Eventually a wheelchair may be in order. Even if your loved one can walk, you may find it easier to stay on schedule with a wheelchair. For example, you may be able to get your loved one into the car for a medical appointment without fussing with the walker, but once you get to the hospital or the doctor's office, things can get complicated quickly. Should you let them start walking inside while you park the car? While you park, will they wander or get lost? Will they stay and wait in the lobby for you? How long will it take for you to find a parking spot and then walk what seems to be ten miles back to the lobby? A wheelchair can help with a number of these issues. If you get your beloved out of the car and into the wheelchair, they are less likely to wander away since you are pushing them, and they have no choice but to stay with you. If the weather is good, you can push them to the appointment. If it is raining or snowing, they can sit in the chair and wait inside while you park.

This is the time to ask the doctor for a handicapped parking sticker or placard. Doctors and their staff are familiar with the paperwork. The doctor may be surprisingly willing to do the paperwork. After you get the placard, parking will be closer to the front door, and your beloved will be alone for less time while you park.

When looking to get a wheelchair, be aware that there are many models and designs. Lightweight models are easier to get out of the trunk or back seat of the car. However, if your loved one is a larger person, they may not be comfortable in a smaller chair. Test several chairs and select the best combination of comfort, portability, and features for your family. Consulting with a physical therapist can be beneficial when fitting your loved one to a wheelchair.

Power Chairs and Scooters

When mobility declines even more, a power chair or scooter becomes a daily-use item. Scooters are commonly seen on sidewalks and in the park, but they don't work particularly well inside smaller spaces. The longer shape and handlebar steering of a scooter makes it difficult to navigate inside. Power chairs may be a better option for sitting at the dinner table, going to the movies, or for just sitting in the living room. Power chairs might be more expensive, but if you struggle to maneuver your beloved long distances, they may be worth the extra cost.

Power chairs and scooters are more difficult to transport. Many models can be broken down into smaller parts, but this process takes time, and some of the parts are heavy. This can be an issue if the caregiver is particularly small or frail. If it is financially possible, a handicapped van with a ramp or lift is a wonderful convenience. If your loved one can no longer drive, a van may be a solution. The ramp or lift will allow you to roll them inside the van, where there is heat and air-conditioning. The ramp or lift makes it easy to strap down the chair and be on your way.

Motor Vehicles

When your loved one is no longer able to drive, it can be a painful time. It is a traumatic transition for both of you. It lays bare the reality of the disease to your loved one, and it increases the burden on you. Before this happened, you could leave work, run over to the doctor's office, meet your beloved and the doctor, and return to work.

Your beloved may fight giving up their driver's license. But you will suspect they can't process all the inputs involved in driving. They may have already been in a fender bender. What if they don't notice the child chasing the ball into the street? What if they are unable to manage the on-ramp, merge into high-speed traffic, or understand the signs telling them when to change lanes for the off-ramp? Inclement weather—either in the north, where the roads get snow-covered or icy, or in the south, where there are heavy rains—poses additional demands on a person's mental capacity. What if they get lost? Do you wait until they wreck the car or drive through the garage door? What if you wait until they cause someone else massive injury or death? These times of transitions are stressful, bordering on traumatic. All these changes will wear on you. You are not the first person who has faced these challenges. Many others have gone through the same struggles.

Everyone wants to maintain their independence until the last possible moment. However, this moment is not as clearly defined as we wish it were. The consequences of waiting too long can be massive. It is better to err on the side of caution and eliminate the loved one's driving earlier than later.

Consider William:

> William was a proud man with a distinguished past. One night he went on a quick errand across town. Six hours later, the sheriff in a neighboring state found him lost in a field. William did not know where he was or how he got there. He was fortunate enough that he was known in the law enforcement community. When the sheriff called his wife at 2 a.m., she had to guarantee the tow bill payment and make separate arrangements for his transportation home. Otherwise, the sheriff would have to place him in jail until someone could come and get him. This incident happened during the summer in the Rocky Mountains. Had it happened in the winter, he would likely have died of exposure.

Consider Wally:

> Wally was not able to drive, yet he still pocketed the keys, possibly out of years of habit or maybe to feel

independent again. Yet when Wendy needed the keys and asked if they were in his pocket, he would swear they were not. She could see the keys making the bulge in his pocket, but his ego or the dementia kept him from knowing the keys were there.

Wendy went to the key shop and got keys that were thrown away. Wendy put these useless keys on Wally's favorite ring so that he could continue to believe he had not lost his independence. At the same time, it gave Wendy peace of mind that Wally was not going to drive and hurt someone.

Other Transportation

Eventually you may have to arrange other transportation. There are, of course, taxis, ride-sharing services such as Uber and Lyft, etc., but they are expensive. However, they are less expensive than killing or maiming someone. Other options might include your church. Sometime a church has volunteers willing to drive members to doctor's offices or on errands. If your beloved is a veteran, the Veteran's Administration (VA) and Disabled American Veterans (DAV) may be able to assist in transporting your loved one. Your town or city may offer Curb-to-Curb buses, sometimes called medi-vans. These special buses are usually operated by the city transportation department. Curb-to-Curb works differently than normal buses. Rather than requiring the rider to walk to the nearest bus stop, these buses come to their homes. Your loved one must be able to exit the residence, make it to the bus, pay the fare, and board. The driver will not likely be able to assist them on or off the bus. With proper notice, some of these buses may be handicapped accessible for a wheelchair, power chair, or scooter. This cost is generally higher than a regular bus, but the convenience is usually worth the additional cost.

Stairs in the Home

As mobility continues to decrease, navigating stairs in an older home can become a problem for your loved one. This can become a barrier to remaining at home, especially if there are living areas on separate floors. If navigating stairs becomes a health risk not worth taking, a stairlift may be an option. These are not something that one purchases at the local hardware store and sets up in an afternoon. This is something that should be installed only by a professional.

Falling and Getting Up

With early falls, your loved one will be able to get up independently. Later, they will require your help. One handy piece of equipment to help them up is a gate belt. Physical therapists use them regularly to ensure a patient's safety. These sturdy plastic belts are placed around a patient's waist and used to help them move, transfer.

To help your beloved get up after a fall, bring a sturdy solid chair close to them. Do not use a rocker, a swivel chair, or any chair with wheels. Strap the gate belt around them and help them maneuver to their hands and knees. Working together, both of you may be able to pull them partially onto the chair. Use the gate belt to assist them onto their feet. Once on their feet, they should rotate to sit in the chair. And after they are on the chair, both the patient and the caregiver should take time to catch their breath.

There is a bigger gate belt, at least eight inches wide, with sturdy grab straps in loops all the way around. This is easier to use when your loved one falls in a corner or confined space. As before, strap the belt on them, and then clear an area where you can assist your loved one to get onto their hands and knees. Together you may be able to get your beloved to crawl out of the smaller space to a chair so they can get to their feet and then rotate to a sitting position.

Hospital Beds

There may come a time when it will be beneficial to order a hospital bed. The higher mattress level makes it easier for the caregiver. Nurses will verify how much the higher bed helps to prevent back injuries. When your loved one moves into a hospital bed, it might also be time to move from the master bedroom to a guest room or another room in the house that is near a bathroom and has more room for the caregiver, walker, wheelchair, and other equipment. Older hospital beds have side rails to help your beloved pull themselves upright. This may help them get to the bathroom quickly, so you can avoid the Blue Glove Club. The rails may also help keep them from falling when trying to get up without help. The ability to raise and lower the bed allows the height to be customized for the patient. The ideal placement is so their feet are flat on the floor when they are sitting upright on the mattress. Too low makes it difficult to get up. If the bed is too high, they have to slide off the mattress to get their feet flat on the floor. The perfect height also makes it easier to get to a standing position and then into a wheelchair or grab a walker.

Fall Alerts and Panic Buttons

When falls become more common, it may wise to get an emergency call device, also known as a panic button. The button can be worn as a lanyard around the neck, around the wrist in a similar be worn like a watch or clipped to clothing. The newer devices have a fall alert. The device can detect a fast change of attitude, and the monitoring system will call to ask the person if they need help. These devices have a monthly charge, but they can provide emotional comfort to the caregiver.

Tracking Devices

When you worry your beloved will wander, consider a tracking device. Like a fall alert, these can be worn around the neck as a lanyard, strapped to the wrist like a watch, or clipped to clothing. The device you select should have a cell tower connection or GPS tracker for patients who wander and can get lost. Costs vary and usually require a subscription. Capabilities are always increasing. Get the best one you can afford. The newest feature may only be used once, but once is all it takes to pay for itself.

If your loved one has a smartphone, you can set a tracking signal to see where they are. It is the location of the phone, but if the phone is in their pocket, it will help. Are they in the house or walking in the park? If they are in the park, have they been stationary for too long? Did they fall?

Another tracking device that has been used successfully is a luggage tracking system such as Google's Tile, Samsung's Galaxy Smart tag system, or Apple's Air Tag. By placing the tracking chip in your beloved's purse or wallet, or even tying it to their shoes or belt, the location of the tag can be tracked in real-time and displayed on a map. Even if the signal is a few minutes old, a search can be narrowed quickly. As above, the peace of mind this can provide is worth as much as the price of the system, especially if your beloved wanders away during times of extreme heat or cold.

Door Alarms

If your beloved wanders in the house, especially at night, a door alarm may be necessary. A string of bells may be enough to tell you they have gone outside. If bells aren't enough, there are several types of reasonably priced door alarms.

Door Locks

If your beloved wants to wander outside, another idea is to add an additional keypad dead bolt on the inside of the door. (The lock is installed backwards.) There is no guarantee this will work, but dementia patients generally have a tough time remembering a sequence of numbers, such as is necessary to unlock the door. This may help keep them in the house while allowing you the freedom to exit, as necessary. You will still need a second regular lock, so strangers cannot just walk into your living room. Another idea is to put an additional lock near the top of the door. A person with dementia will often not be able to figure out a second lock.

Lost Item Trackers

Another irritation is the constant hunting for misplaced things. Eyeglasses, TV remotes, expensive phones, and hearing aids all get misplaced. You can purchase electronic locators that can be stuck to the things you search for the most. They come with a remote that causes a locator to chirp when activated. These systems come with various features based on their price. Your sanity may be worth the cost of one.

Telephones

As the disease progresses, patients become less and less adept at using technology. Images on a screen may confuse them; they may not understand the connection between pressing a button and the result. To keep your beloved calm and yet give them a sense of independence, a simple prepaid cell phone, sometimes called a burner phone, can work. The phone can be programmed so the patient can make a call by pressing only one button on the keypad. You may want to program this phone to call your number. Or, if your loved one is calling you at 2:00 a.m. wanting ice cream, you may want every preprogrammed number to be the main number for the facility's switchboard. Another advantage is, if the facility is complaining about your beloved calling excessively, you can let the prepaid minutes run out. Additionally, you can make an excuse that you need to physically take the phone to the store to add airtime. This will allow you to check what numbers your loved one has called. More important, you will know who has been calling your beloved. Some of these phones offer the option to disable outgoing calls. If scam callers become a problem, the phone number can be changed for a minimal charge.

Telephone scams from bad actors cost US citizens over $30 billion a year (https://www.cnbc.com/2021/06/29/). These bad actors focus on states with a large population of senior citizens. It is difficult to spot spoofing as the call will appear to come in from a local area code and phone number. The offer to extend an auto warranty or provide technical support for a computer is difficult for a dementia patient to refuse. Even worse is when the caller uses intimidation and fear. They engage your loved one by stating they are from the Internal Revenue Service, Social Security, or the local police department, and insist on immediate payment. Giving a credit card number over the phone causes no end of problems for the caregiver. It may best to remove the credit card from their wallet with a therapeutic fiblet such as the card is being reissued.

Because of their reduced mental capacity, dementia patients can be more trusting and therefore more susceptible to telephone scams. A common scam involving the elderly is for the scammer to pose as the grandchild of an elderly person. The scammer will call and explain to "grandma" that they are in trouble and they need some financial help. They will generally include the phrase "don't tell mom and dad." At this point the scammer passes the phone to an accomplice who pretends to be the grandchild's attorney. The accomplice then explains how much trouble the phony grandchild is in and how the problem can be resolved by sending money to a third party. This will be accompanied by a fantastic story about how the attorney has worked with the court to get the grandchild released if only they can pay the phony fine or post the phony bail by the end of the day. A person with dementia might not have a grandchild, but they could still respond to an appeal from a scammer saying they need a new Medicare card, or the energy company saying their bill is not paid and they will cut off their power unless there is a payment by the end of the day. Perhaps the scammer will offer a huge prize, but they will need to verify the social security number, birthdate etc.

For reasons like this it is a good idea to keep track of not only the beloved's outgoing calls but the incoming calls as well.

Stories of dementia patients calling 911 from an assisted-living or a memory-care facility are legendary. Many 911 dispatch offices have the local nursing facilities' main numbers and will call the switchboard prior to dispatching an ambulance.

The Kitchen

The kitchen is a source of all types of dangers, from the hot stove to silverware and kitchen knives. A dementia patient who was a professional chef will want his own knives and to continue to cook meals for the family. The caregiver will never be able to cook and season food as well as the chef. But the day will come when it is not safe for your beloved chef to be in the kitchen. Shortly after that, making coffee and boiling liquids will not be safe. When your beloved becomes belligerent, everyday forks and knives will become dangerous.

Willis and Wanda had been married for fifty-one years.

> She suffered from sundowners and was jealous and belligerent with Willis for having a best friend. (The men had been friends for decades.) At dinner, Wanda took a knife from the table and stabbed Willis in the hand, breaking the skin and requiring a trip to the emergency department. She was never again allowed to cut her own food or use anything but a spoon.

Cabinet Locks

Because your beloved is losing the ability to remember and is effectively going backward in age, it may be necessary to install baby locks on cabinets, especially those that store chemicals, drugs, or power tools.

Sharp tools such as knives, scissors, razors, haircutting equipment, and nail clippers should be removed not only from the reach of a loved one with dementia but from their sight as well. Keeping these sharp tools out of reach is important because a dementia patient will not recognize their loss of ability and will likely continue to use these common items as though nothing is wrong until something goes horribly wrong. Toenail and fingernail trimming should be done by a family member or professional. A side benefit is that your beloved may enjoy the attention of someone besides their caregiver.

Cooking

As the disease progresses, you may have to make more food preparations before leaving your loved one alone. Microwaves are safer than a stove or oven as they turn themselves off. Single-serving microwave meals are reasonably priced and easy for your beloved to manage. A selection of microwave meals may allow them to prepare their own meals and help them maintain their independence for a while longer.

However, if your beloved is home alone, they may decide to cook. Possibly they are hungry for something special for lunch, or maybe they want to surprise you with dinner when you get home. A simple and free solution is to take the knobs off the stove. Keep the knobs in your purse, in a different room, inside a pot that isn't used often, or in a top cabinet they can't reach. This will keep the stove and oven turned off. Another free option is to turn off the stove circuit breaker. Additionally, there are appliance monitors that detect if the stove or oven has been left on for too long.

Cameras

Home security system cameras can be an inexpensive way to monitor your beloved while you are away.

Dean was still working an eight to five job and was a few years from retirement,

He had to keep working those last few years to get his pension check. But dementia forced his wife, Diane, to quit her job. She was home alone all day. With only one paycheck coming in, there wasn't enough money to hire a sitter. While Dean was at work, he worried about her. He installed security cameras to allow him to watch her activities from his smartphone. These paid for themselves one time when Dean observed her fall from his office. He was able to coach her onto the couch through the voice function on the camera. Dean thought this was a good setup until Diane resented being watched, so she tottered on a chair and took the cameras down. You should be laughing. All she needed to do was unplug them. Laughing is so much better than the frustration Dean was feeling.

Firearms and Power Tools

Regardless of one's opinion on private ownership of firearms, safe storage of firearms, ammunition, and other implements that could be used against the caregiver should be carefully considered. A person with dementia has diminished mental capacity and may not recognize their caregiver and believe the caregiver is an intruder. It may be appropriate to sell or give away these items. If the idea of parting with these is too difficult, it may be wise to invest in a biometric safe, remote storage, or a hidden key as part of an overall safety and security plan. A fiblet may be necessary to get your beloved to allow their firearms to be locked down. Failing this, it may be possible to hide the ammunition and replace it with inert ammunition. If you are uncomfortable with any of these processes, consult a gunsmith or shooting sports facility.

For power tools, some things to consider are: For large tools such as table saws, unplug or disable the circuit breaker. For corded tools, cut the plug off close to the plug end. It can be replaced later. For cordless tools, remove and hide the batteries. For hand tools, a locking toolbox may be required.

Shaving

Hygiene in men can be accomplished with an electric shaver rather than a blade. They will complain that the shave is not as close as a blade. Just be ready for it. A fiblet may be in order. Something like this might work: "You must use an electric shaver temporarily because of a strike at the blade factory."

A Loving Heart

Before we leave the subject of equipment, remember these are suggestions for the caregiver. They don't substitute for having a loving heart and a caring soul. These ideas and techniques are included to make your life easier. Use them or modify them to suit your unique circumstances. None of these ideas can replace you and your loving heart.

CHAPTER 24

Xtras

To properly care for your loved one, you must keep yourself in top condition. This includes physically, mentally, spiritually, and emotionally. Caregiving will take a toll on you. There is no way that it cannot. *Caregiving in the U.S. 2020* found that nearly 25 percent of caregivers ignore their own health, and their health is getting worse. Exhausted caregivers suffer from depression, anxiety, and anger. Peter Vitaliano, a professor of geriatric psychiatry at the University of Washington and an expert on caregiving, said that the chronic stress of caring for someone can lead to high blood pressure, diabetes, and a compromised immune system. Elderly caregivers are at a 63 percent higher risk of mortality than noncaregivers in the same age group, according to a study by University of Pittsburgh in December 1999 (https://www.brmmlaw.com/blog/2014/september/70-of-all-caregivers-over-the-age-of-70-die-firs/).

Remember that you are your beloved's best and most important asset. You must maintain yourself in the best possible physical condition. This includes having a healthy diet, an exercise routine, and getting sufficient sleep.

Beyond your physical body, you need to keep your physical environment maintained. This includes your home and its support systems. The furnace filter needs changed, the gutters need cleaned, the lawn needs to be mowed, and in the winter, if you live in a northern climate, the walks may need to be shoveled. All these daily obligations remain while you take care of your beloved. If these systems fail, your caregiving efforts will be negatively affected.

Your transportation (car, truck, SUV, van) must be well maintained. Keeping the car filled with fuel seems obvious, but it's easy to forget to fill the tank when you are distracted by caring for your loved one. A monthly trip to a favored mechanic for a "once over" including oil level, tire pressure, washer fluid, coolant level, etc., will buy peace of mind and may avoid a potential emergency.

Adult day care or a personal companion may be appropriate for your beloved and give you a chance to go to the gym or get away for a few hours. These are not inexpensive, but they are less expensive than having your beloved in long-term care and you, the caregiver, in intensive care.

CHAPTER 25

Yes, It Will Happen to You

Dealing with dementia can be analogous to going to war. For example, everyone who goes to war thinks they will survive. They also think they will return home unchanged. But no one returns from a war zone without profound changes in the way they think, feel, act, and remember. Everyone who helps a loved one during a long-term illness is profoundly changed by the experience. No matter how much reading, research, or studying you do, the illness will hit you in ways and places you never expected. And there is nothing you can do about this.

You will ride the ups and downs of dementia days with the rest of us. Just when you adjust to the new normal, the latest wonder medication will stop working, and you will be back in free fall. No one knows when it will occur. But it will; that is guaranteed.

Burnout is a real issue with caregiving. Even with the best intentions, caregivers can miss things. You are tempted to delay getting small things done as the recent complaint isn't urgent. But the patient may feel differently. Once a dementia patient gets a thought in their mind, it tends to stay there. Their ability to think through a situation is diminished. This diminished capacity can lead to disaster.

Mom was elderly and lived with her daughter, Yvette.

Mom was in and out of awareness and occasionally would recognize how stressed her daughter had become. Yvette knew that her mom should have her nails trimmed professionally, but she was overwhelmed by the demands at work. One day, because her nails had grown so long, and she decided she couldn't wait any longer, mom got the toenail clippers and began to chop at her nails. When Yvette got home from work, she found bloody footprints all over the kitchen floor. Mom had cut her nails and skin so deeply that a trip to the emergency department was required. After some stitches, she was discharged. Yvette was forced to take even more time off work as mom could hardly walk the next day. When Yvette had a few minutes, she searched for and found all the nail clippers, files, and scissors and hid them.

It is easy to become overwhelmed with demands, requests, needs, and desires. But *you* are the most valuable resource your loved one has. *You cannot* do this alone. This bears repeating: *You cannot* do this alone! If *you* try to go it alone, *you* run a significant risk of killing *yourself* before your loved one dies.

CHAPTER 26

ZZZ: Sleeping Is So Important

ZZZ is for sleep. The more sleep you get, the more you *can* sleep. When you are beyond exhausted, you will find it hard to get to sleep and harder to stay asleep. And when you are caretaking, you will tend to listen for your loved one. Do they toss and turn? If they are restless sleepers or use a noisy Cpap machine, you may choose to sleep in a different room. Forget what the neighbors say. Forget what the kids think. You need to be able to sleep long enough and well enough to be rested for the next day. Your loved one may also sleep better alone. Maybe you are the one who needs the Cpap machine, and the noise is keeping them awake. Do what works for your situation.

In Zola's case, her husband had a stroke that caused the dementia symptoms.

His limited mobility mandated a hospital bed. The hospital bed didn't fit into the bedroom and had to go into the living room. Using the bed required a higher bedside table, different sheets and blankets, different lamps and other bedroom accessories. The hospital bed changed everything. Zola would get up several times a night to check on him, to listen to ensure he was still breathing. Looking back, she felt so silly! If he was breathing, why did she interrupt her own sleep? If he wasn't breathing, there was probably nothing that could be done. When she realized this, she went back to bed and slept soundly for the next several hours.

Still, we listen for our loved ones during the night. It is common for dementia patients to get more confused at night. Loved ones wonder if they are up using the bathroom. Are they in the right room? Patients have been known to urinate on the living room chair, thinking it was the toilet. After all, the chair was white and about the right height.

None of this is news to you. Everything associated with your loved one involves *you*, *your* watchfulness, *your* time, and *your* energy. All this effort saps your strength, exhausting you. Exhausted as you are, you still can't sleep. You lay your head down, but your mind goes over and over all the nuances, all the behaviors, all the changes. You try to predict what is yet to come. How are you going to manage the next step? How long can you survive financially? What about your health insurance? If you quit your job to care for your loved one, the group health insurance will disappear. If neither of you is old enough for Medicare and you quit, there may not be any health insurance. No, you can't quit! But your loved one needs more care. But you are vested in your own retirement and could retire in just a few more years. You'd never be able to work long enough to do so at another company. If you quit now, will you have enough money to survive when you retire? Over and over, your mind churns with options, strategies, and choices. By the morning, you are exhausted, have no more clarity than last night, and you still must get up.

How do you know you're exhausted? It starts early in your day when the alarm clock goes off. You sleep through the first couple of rings. You want to stay in bed, pull the covers over your head, and avoid the day. Then when you do get up, your eyes are tired and scratchy. You head for the bathroom, and though you're too tired to shower, you must for your coworkers' sakes. You stand in the shower with your eyes closed and think about what to make for breakfast. You know they will want waffles, but you don't want to cook waffles. Hopefully, they will settle for instant grits. You are so tired! The water feels so good! Then you realize you don't have time to make breakfast! Caregiving is tough on sleeping.

Some nights, Zeb couldn't recognize the door to the bathroom.

> He would go outside and pee on his favorite bush. This led to a myriad of issues. Would the neighbors call the police? Would Zeb be charged with indecent exposure?

> One winter night, his wife found him outside, barefoot in the snow, looking for that favorite bush. But it was covered with snow, so he didn't recognize it. For his safety and her peace of mind, she had to alarm all the doors. She slept better, but better isn't always enough. This poor wife was always sleeping with one ear open. But now at least, she was only listening for the loud alarm, not the soft sound of the door closing.

Try to take a nap when your loved one is napping. The dishes will still be dirty when you get up. Yes, the laundry will get wrinkled in the dryer. But take that nap anyway. You can soak the dishes and turn the dryer back on to get rid of the wrinkles ... later. Right now, lie down for a while. Put your feet up. Sleep if you can. You need to be rested for the struggle to get them to swallow those pills and for you to answer that same question for the thousandth time. And more important, to tell them how much they are loved.

AFTERWORD

Just before this book went to the publisher, we went through the trauma of dementia again. We got to go through what you are going through—again. We again are dealing with the belligerence, helplessness, and obstructive family members.

Again, we dealt with the insurance and long-term care paperwork. We have again been exhausted by the demands of the disease and the helpless medical industry to deal with dementia. All this compounded by our other life obligations.

Even though we have given you our best ideas, tips, and suggestions, we know from experience that nothing, not even having been through it before, can prepare one for the universal struggle this disease brings. Take what we have offered you and use what you can. Discard the rest and do your best with a loving heart and a caring soul. You have our respect and blessing.

From one caregiver to another, we wish you the best.

Mike and Patrice
Christmas 2022

GLOSSARY

Abstractions: The ability to group things or concepts into categories. For example, knowing that a banana and an apple are both fruits.

Activities of Daily Living (ADLs): Five basic activities considered necessary for independent living at home or in the community. They include personal hygiene, dressing, eating, continence, and transferring/ mobility.

Alzheimer's Disease: The most common type of dementia, with a continuous decline in thinking and behavioral and social skills that affect a person's ability to function independently.

Anosognosia: A condition or symptom that causes a patient to be unaware of their status. For example, a frail ninety-year-old man requiring a walker insisting on trying to rototill the garden.

Anger Multidimensional Anger Inventory (MAI): Thirty-eight questions based on psychologist Judith Siegel's work in determining anger dimensions, developed in 1986.

Aphasia, Progressive Non Fluent (PNFA): A gradual degrading of verbal fluency where patients struggle to form words and make grammar errors. Generally, patients retain their comprehension, causing additional frustration.

Assessment before Acceptance: An evaluation required before admission into assisted-living facilities and nursing homes. Legally, facilities cannot accept patients whose needs are more than they can provide.

Assisted Living Facility (ALF or AL): A facility that combines room and board with medical and personal care. The family must furnish the patient's room.

Baseline: A patient's level of physical and/or mental compromise when first diagnosed. It is the point where decline is first measured.

Beneficiary Designations: A person who will directly receive the proceeds of certain funds, such as bank accounts or insurance proceeds.

Blue Glove Club: The club no one wants to join, involving latex gloves and the personal hygiene of your beloved.

Delayed Recall: A common test of dementia's progress where patients are required to repeat a list of three items after fifteen minutes. If the patient can't remember any of the words, they are in the end of the moderate stage and entering the severe stage.

Delirium: When patients see or hear things others do not. It can also include restlessness, pacing, drumming of fingers, or speaking incoherently.

Dementia: A group of mental conditions that interfere with the tasks of daily living. Dementia is not diagnosed unless there is impairment of at least two brain functions, such as memory loss and judgment.

Dementia, Alzheimer's Disease (ALZ): The most common type of dementia, with a continuous decline in thinking, behavioral, and social skills that affect a person's ability to function independently.

Dementia, Cortical: Dementia damage to the outer layer of the brain. Usual symptoms show up as memory and language problems.

Dementia, Frontotemporal (FTD): A group of diseases characterized by the breakdown of nerve cells and their connections in the frontal and temporal lobes of the brain. Common symptoms affect behavior, personality changes, thinking, judgment, language, and movement.

Dementia, Lewy Body: Lewy bodies are abnormal balloon-like clumps of protein that have been found in the brains of affected people. This is the third most common type of dementia. Common signs are visual hallucinations and problems with focus and attention.

Dementia, Life Expectancy by Type:

Dementia Type	Life Expectancies
Alzheimer's Disease	Ten years following diagnosis
Vascular Dementia	Five years following diagnosis
Dementia with Lewy Bodies	Two to eight years following pronounced symptoms

Dementia, Mixed: Dementia developed from a combination of causes, such as Alzheimer's disease and Lewy body dementia. These patients may have exhibited symptoms of memory loss, coordination problems, and/or hallucinations.

Dementia Rating, Clinical (CDR): Another system to rate dementia, CDR is a five-point system based on cognitive abilities and how well a person functions in six areas: memory, orientation, judgment and problem-solving, community affairs, home and hobbies, and personal care. Based on interviews with the subject and others, including family members, one of five possible stages is assigned.

(Clinical) Dementia Rating (CDR) Scale

Stage	Description	Expected Duration of Stage
CDR-0	Very mild dementia: Memory problems are slight, but consistent.	N/A
CDR-0.5	Some difficulty with time and problem-solving. Daily life is slightly impaired. Individuals can perform personal care activities	Average duration is up to seven years.
CDR-1	Mild dementia: Memory loss is moderate, especially for recent events, and interferes with daily activities. Moderate difficulty with solving problems. Cannot function independently at community affairs. Difficulty with daily activities and hobbies, especially complex ones.	Average duration is two years.
CDR-2	Moderate dementia: More profound memory loss, only retaining highly learned material. Disorientation with respect to time and place. Impaired judgment, with difficulty handling problems. Little to no independent function at home. Can only do simple chores. Fewer interests.	Average duration is just under two years to four years.
CDR-3	Severe dementia: Severe memory loss. Disorientation with respect to time or place. No judgment or problem-solving abilities. Cannot participate in community affairs outside the home. Requires help with all tasks of daily living. Requires help with most personal care. Frequent incontinence.	Average duration is one year to two and a half years.

Dementia, Subcortical: Dementia caused by damage to the inner (deeper) layers of the brain. Usual symptoms include forgetfulness and slowed thinking.

Dementia, Vascular: Second most common type of dementia, caused by damage to the vessels that supply blood to the brain. Blood vessel problems can cause strokes or affect the brain in other ways, such as by damaging the white matter of the brain due to reduced blood supply. The most common signs of vascular dementia include difficulties with problem-solving, slowed thinking, and loss of focus and organization.

Denial: An unconscious defense mechanism. An individual in denial is unable or will refuse to recognize or acknowledge objective facts or experiences. They falsely believe this will protect them from the reality of a situation.

Discharge Planner: A social worker who assists the patient and family on what is appropriate when the patient is leaving the hospital.

Doctors (MD), Nurse Practitioners (NP), and Physician Assistants (PA): Medical personnel you will encounter during the medical journey. Doctor's orders are directives to lab tests, X-rays, pharmacy orders, and so on. Nurse practitioners and physician assistants each have less authority than doctors but can order tests, blood work, and prescribe medications.

Do Not Resuscitate Order (DNR): Also known as a "no code," the DNR is a legal document that stops first responders from administering CPR if the patient's heart stops beating. It also lists other medical and technological interventions the patient may or may not want.

Durable Power of Attorney (DPOA): A legal document empowering a person to immediately to act on behalf of another person (generally the patient) who executed the document. A DPOA continues in effect through sickness, accidents, dementia, etc. It may or may not extend to making medical decisions. See Medical Power of Attorney.

Estate Planning Attorney: An attorney who specializes in end-of-life legal matters such as wills, probate, DNRs, and trusts.

Executor or Executrix: The person responsible for ensuring the terms detailed in a will are followed. This person may also be called a personal representative.

Exhaustion, Caregiver: A common condition among those responsible for the care of individuals with chronic and debilitating illnesses. Because of the time and energy required, the caregiver may become injured or the caregiver's family may experience financial stress or emotional dysfunction.

Fiblet, (therapeutic fiblet): A little white lie that makes the patient more compliant and makes the caregiver's day a little easier. It may be easier to change the subject immediately afterwards.

Functional Assessment Staging Test (FAST): A scale that describes the stages of Alzheimer's dementia. It is based more on one's level of functioning and ability to perform activities of daily living than on cognitive decline.

Stage	Patient Condition	Level of Functional Decline	Expected Duration of Stage
1	Normal adult	No functional decline.	N/A
2	Normal older adult	Personal awareness of some functional decline	Unknown.
3	Early Alzheimer's disease	Noticeable deficits in demanding situations.	Average duration of this stage is seven years.
4	Mild Alzheimer's	Requires assistance in complicated tasks such as handling finances, traveling, or planning parties.	Average duration of this stage is two years.

5	Moderate Alzheimer's	Requires assistance in choosing proper clothing.	Average duration of this stage is eighteen months.
6	Moderately severe Alzheimer's	Requires assistance with dressing, bathing, and toileting. Experiences urinary and fecal incontinence.	Average duration of this stage is three and a half months to nine and a half months.
7	Severe Alzheimer's	Speech ability declines to about a half-dozen intelligible words. Progressive loss of the abilities to walk, sit up, smile, and hold head up.	Average duration of this stage is short, less than one year.

Hallucinations: Perceptions of stimuli that don't exist. For example, seeing a locomotive in the house or hearing music that is not playing.

Hospice: A facility that offers end-of-life care that is focused on comfort, not treatment.

Hydrocephalus: A condition characterized by excess fluid in the brain. Blood may leak into the brain of a stroke victim. Adults may suffer chronic headache, nausea, focus, difficulty in walking, drowsiness, changes in personality, seizures.

Illusions: Real stimuli that are misinterpreted. For example, a dark mat in front of a door is misinterpreted as a hole in the floor.

Insurance, Long-Term Care: Private insurance is often used to pay for room and board and other expenses not covered by Medicare. Generally, this insurance is purchased before age sixty, and like most other insurance, is private pay.

Insurance, Medicaid: A government-funded health insurance program for low-income individuals. If the family is transitioning from Medicare to Medicaid, a Medicaid consultant may be helpful.

Insurance, Medicare: A common insurance program for most US citizens after the age of sixty-five. Medicare covers such things as doctor's visits, medication, and hospital stays, but it generally does not cover long-term care expenses such as room and board.

Insurance, Private: Insurance offered by employers or purchased privately by individuals.

Joint Ownership: A legal form of ownership of property, commonly used for property such as homes or vehicles. During the patient's lifetime, the joint owner has the same rights as the patient. After death, property with joint ownership may be given directly to the survivor without going through the probate court process.

Long-Term Care Facilities: Facilities that provide a variety of medical and personal care services to people unable to live independently. These facilities can be costly for the family as the cost is not eligible for Medicare funding.

Major Neurocognitive Disorders: An umbrella term for a group of symptoms caused by damage to the brain, including Alzheimer's, stroke, Parkinson's, multiple sclerosis, dementia, injuries, concussions, infections, and long-term drug or alcohol use.

Medicaid: A government-funded health insurance program for low-income individuals. If the family is transitioning from Medicare to Medicaid, a Medicaid consultant may be helpful.

Medicare: A common insurance program for most US citizens after the age of sixty-five. Medicare covers such things as doctor's visits, medication, and hospital stays but generally does not cover long-term care expenses such as room and board.

Medical Power Of Attorney (MPOA): An MPOA allows an individual to appoint someone else (the agent) to make health-care decisions for them when the individual becomes incapable of making their own health care decisions. An MPOA may be referred to as an advanced health-care directive.

Memory Care Facilities or Memory Care Center (MCF or MCC): Facilities specifically designed and staffed to deal with issues related to dementia. The staff are specifically trained to communicate with the residents, watch for depression or withdrawal, and encourage socialization. Generally, this is an inpatient facility, likely locked, as additional supervision is required.

Mild Cognitive Impairment: A condition causing memory or other thinking problems greater than considered normal for a person's age and education, but not as severe as those seen in people with dementia.

Mini Mental State Exam (MMS): A quick, thirty-point questionnaire used to measure cognitive states for patients suspected of having dementia.

Nurse, Director of (DON): The charge nurse at a given facility who supervises nursing staff, audits medications, and watches over patient progress.

Nurse, Registered (RN), Licensed Practical (LPN), Vocational Practical (VPN): Three types of nurses you are likely to encounter during your dementia journey. RNs have more education and certifications than the others. Jointly, these nurses provide and manage most of the medical care.

Nurse Aides or Certified Nursing Assistants (CNA): These professionals provide most of the hands-on care for your loved one. They are responsible for patient comfort and hygiene.

Obsessive Compulsive Behaviors (OCB): Behaviors such as hoarding, repeatedly asking the same question, or compulsive organizing, that are not necessarily a trait of dementia. OCB can become more pronounced with dementia because of reduced mental capacity in the patient.

Parkinson's Disease: A medical condition that often leads to the development of dementia-like symptoms, as Parkinson's and dementia are related.

Parrots: Friends and family who offer well-meaning, though potentially detrimental, advice. Advice from Parrots can be ignored.

Peacocks: Seemingly cheerful people who want to know how things are so they can inappropriately gossip about your loved one to others.

Personal Representative (PR): See Executor or Executrix.

Physical Health: The most accurate predictor of dementia health. Temporary physical illness can worsen dementia symptoms. Dementia symptoms often subside when the patient becomes physically well.

Primary Care Provider (PCP): The patient's main medical provider. It can be a physician, nurse practitioner, or physician assistant.

Probate: The legal court process where a will is administered and overseen by a probate court judge. This process generally takes six to twelve months.

Power of Attorney (POA): A legal authorization that gives a designated person, termed the attorney-in-fact, the power to act for another person.

Social Workers and Discharge Planners: Discharge planners assist patients and families leaving the hospital. This may include directing them toward a long-term treatment facility, rehabilitation facility, or home. Discharge planners are frequently social workers.

Seagulls: Friends and family who fly in to visit for short periods. They criticize everything the caregiver says and does, thereby diminishing the trust built with the patient and the rest of the family. Seagulls leave the caregivers to pick up the pieces when they return to their ordinary lives.

Semantic Clues: Verbal clues to help your loved one remember things.

Showtiming: When a dementia patient can be witty and charming for a short time, such as at a doctor's appointment. The patient will then be exhausted and will return to their dementia behaviors.

Sundowning: A neurological phenomenon associated with increased confusion and restlessness in people with delirium or some form of dementia. Sundowning may not necessarily be related to the sun, rather fatigue or exhaustion in afternoon and evening.

Technicians: People trained in a specific area, such as X-ray technicians, pharmacy technicians, respiratory therapists, and phlebotomists (blood draw). They relay information to the doctors and the nurses.

Transfer on Death Authorization (TOD): When added to bank accounts, stock accounts, or in some states, real property deeds, that provide for, on the holder's death, the money (or property) to be given directly to the person listed without going through the probate court process.

Traumatic Brain Injury (TBI): Injuries caused when the head hits a hard object, as in a car accident, or through repetitive trauma, such as in boxing that cause brain tissue damage. Depending on what part of the brain is affected, dementia-type symptoms can present.

Trusts: A legal entity created to own and distribute property. Trusts are particularly important if you have a medical history that may cause you to become incapacitated. Trusts have the added benefit of avoiding probate court.

Urinary Tract Infections (UTIs): Common conditions in both men and women with dementia. They should be treated immediately and aggressively as they can worsen symptoms of dementia.

Vultures: Friends and family who want possessions or money. They will not help with the patient or the patient's care, but they will be there to collect their share of the estate when the patient passes away.

Will: A legal document that specifies the distribution of your property, guardianship of your minor children, and other wishes you may have regarding your estate. Wills are supervised by the probate court and usually take a year to complete with the associated expenses. Every adult should have a Will.

SOURCES

Abstractions:
https://www.cdc.gov/aging/dementia/index.html.

Activities of Daily Living (ADLs):
https://findanyanswer.com/what-are-the-5-activities-of-daily-living.

Alzheimer's Disease:
https://www.mayoclinic.org/diseases-conditions/dementia/
symptoms-causes/.

Anger Inventory (MAI):
https://www.idrlabs.com/anger/test.php.

Borderline Unspecified Dementia:
https://www.cdc.gov/aging/dementia/index.html.

Burnout of Caregivers:
https://www.verywellhealth.com/signs-of-caregiver-burnout-97981

Care Needs at Each Stage:
https://www.dementiacarecentral.com/caregiverinfo/
memory-problems/.

Caregiving in the US 2020:
https://www.brmmlaw.com/blog/2014/september/70-of-all-caregiver
s-over-the-age-of-70-die-firs/.

Chronic Stress:
https://www.brmmlaw.com/blog/2014/september/70-of-all-caregiver
s-over-the-age-of-70-die-first.

Cost of Dementia Care:
http://www.rand.org/pubs/external_publications/EP50247.html.

Delayed Recall:
https://www.cdc.gov/aging/dementia/index.html.

Delirium:
https://www.cdc.gov/aging/dementia/index.html.

Dementia:
https://www.webmd.com/alzheimers/types-dementia#1.

Dementia, Frontotemporal (FTD):
https://www.dementiacarecentral.com/aboutdementia/
frontotemporal/.

Dementia Rating, Clinical:
https://www.dementiacarecentral.com/aboutdementia/diagnosing/.

Elder Law on Durable Power of Attorney Documents:
https://www.elderlawanswers.com/the-durable-power-o
f-attorney-12041.

Life Expectancy by Dementia Type:
https://www.dementiacarecentral.com/.

Mass General Brigham on Advanced Care Directives: https://
www.brighamandwomensfaulkner.org/patients-and-families/
advance-care-directives/dnr-orders.

Multidimensional Anger Test:

https://www.verywellhealth.com/
anger-and-aggression-in-dementia-4134488.

Nolo Company:
https://www.nolo.com/legal-encyclopedia/probate-faq.html.

Rand Corporation:
https://www.rand.org/pubs/external_publications/EP50247.html.

Understanding Relationship Dynamics:
https://drdenisenadler.com/what-are-relationship-dynamics/.

REFERENCES

Abbit, Linda. *The Conscious Caregiver*. Adams Media, Simon and Schuster, 2017.

Beattie, Melody. *The Language of Letting Go*. MJF Books, 1990.

Best, Suzanne. *Love Our Vets with PTSD*. Deep River Books, 2015.

Bradshaw, John. *Home Coming*. New York: Bantom Books, 1990.

Buscaglia, Leo. *Bus 9 to Paradise*. Slack Inc., 1986.

Buscaglia, Leo. *Living, Loving & Learning*. New York: Ballantine Books, 1982.

Buscaglia, Leo. *Love, What Life Is All About*. New York: Ballantine Books, 1972.

Carnage, Dale. *How to Win Friends and Influence People*. Flash Books, 1937.

Champlin, Joseph. *Through Death to Life*. Ave Maria Press, 2002.

Christensen, Andre, and Neil Jacobson. *Reconcilable Differences*. Guilford Press, 2000.

Cohen, Alan. *I Had It All the Time*, Alan Cohen Publishing, 1995.

Covey, Stephen. *7 Habits of Highly Effective People*. New York: Fireside Book, Simon and Schuster, 1990.

Creek, Humble. *Light for My Path*. Barbour, 1999.

Dunn, Hank. *Hard Choices for Loving People*. A&A Publishers, 2009.

Fishel, Ruth. *Time for Joy*. Health Communications, 1988.

Grabhorn, Lynn. *Excuse Me, Your Life is Waiting*. Hampton Roads, 2012.

Grunwald, Lisa. *Whatever Makes You Happy*. New York: Random House, 2005.

Gungor, Mark. *Laugh Your Way to a Better Marriage*. Atria Paperback, 2008.

Joseph, Jenny. *When I Am an Old Woman, I Shall Wear Purple*, ed. Sandra Martz. Papier-Mache Press, 1987.

Kabat-Zinn, Jon. *Mindfulness Based Stress Reduction*. Palouse Mindfulness, 1987.

Kingma, Daphne. *Coming Apart*. MJF Books, 1987.

Kornfield, Jack. *After the Ecstasy, the Laundry*. New York: Bantam Books, 2000.

Mace, Nancy, and Peter Rabins. *The 36-Hour Day*. Grand Central Life and Style, 2011.

Manning, Doug. *Share My Lonesome Valley: The Slow Grief of Long-term Care*. In Sight Books, 2001.

Manning, Doug. *When Love Gets Tough, The Nursing Home Decision*. In Sight Books, 2006.

Mother Theresa. *Do Something Beautiful for God*. Blue Sparrow, Dynamic Catholic, 2020.

Seahorn, Janet, and Anthony Seahorn. *Tears of a Warrior*. Team Pursuits, 2008.

Smedes, Lewis. *Forgive and Forget*. New York: Harper and Row, 1987.

Sparks, Nicholas. *The Notebook*. Warner Books, 2004.

Tierney, Elizabeth. *Dignifying Dementia*. Oak Tree Press, 2011.

Tolle, Eckhart. *The Power of Now*. New World Library, 1999.

Warren, Rick. *The Purpose Driven Life*. Grand Rapids, MI: Zondervan, 2002.

Wolfelt, Alan. *Understanding Your Grief*. Companion Press, 2003.

ABOUT THE AUTHORS

Patrice Gapen was a college instructor of computer science for most of her life, writing fourteen textbooks with her co-authors. Her greatest joy in life was and is teaching. She has taught people to program computers and fly airplanes and is a parent and grandmother.

For most of his life, Michael Hand was an engineer specializing in the construction of dams and reservoirs. He cared for his wife during her battle with dementia while juggling the duties of an engineer for four long years.

Printed in the United States
by Baker & Taylor Publisher Services